W9-CMV-540

8/6

THE
QUEEN'S
SILVER

GEORGIUS TERTIUS
DEI GRATIÂ BRITANNIARUM REX.
PATER PATRIÆ.

see page 104

By Gracious Permission of Her Majesty Queen Elizabeth II

THE QUEEN'S SILVER

A Survey of Her Majesty's Personal Collection

by A. G. GRIMWADE

London THE CONNOISSEUR 1953

First published 1953
Designed and produced for
THE CONNOISSEUR
by Rainbird, McLean Ltd, London
Set in Monotype Plantin with Gresham initials
and printed in Great Britain by The Westerham Press Ltd.
Blocks by Austin Miles Ltd.
Bound by James Burn Ltd.

CONTENTS

The Text   *page* 1

The Plates   *page* 55

LIST OF PLATES

All from photographs by Messrs A. C. Cooper Ltd

FOREWORD

THE silver illustrated and described in the pages which follow has been selected from the personal collection of plate jointly belonging to Her Majesty the Queen and His Royal Highness the Duke of Edinburgh. It was in use at Clarence House, London, from the time of Her Majesty's marriage until her departure for Buckingham Palace after her accession to the throne. The publishers acknowledge with gratitude the gracious permission given them to spread a wider knowledge of Her Majesty's personal plate. They are especially mindful of the help and facilities so readily accorded by General Sir Frederick Browning for a detailed examination of this silver and acknowledge, also, the patient assistance of Mr E. Bennett, Her Majesty's butler, in connection with its photography. Finally, certain of the identifications of coat-of-arms on pieces in the collection have been kindly supplied by Mr Leslie G. Pine, managing editor of *Burke's Peerage*.

December 1952

L. G. G. RAMSEY
Editor, *The Connoisseur*

THE QUEEN'S SILVER

SINCE the days of the Pharaohs and Sea Kings of Crete the precious metals have exerted their hold on man and contributed very largely to his expressions of power and security. In the form of wrought vessels for his personal use or of jewellery and regalia for his adornment, they have been heaped century after century into treasuries of church and state to be dispersed and reacquired by new owners or broken up, melted down and re-formed to suit the changing fashions of a succeeding generation. The burial customs of pagan civilisations have joined forces with the curiosity of antiquarians or chance discovery to bring to light brief glimpses of the store the ancients set on their possessions, the intricacy of their design and the skill of unknown craftsmen. From pyramids, caves, Saxon ship burials, and even the bare earth turned up by the plough, we add to our modern treasures the creations of past ages in this and other lands. At any moment another Sutton Hoo or Mildenhall may offer up its secrets and close the gap in our knowledge of some age of our artistic inheritance yet scarcely appreciated. Once the dark ages are passed and the Gothic world is reached our knowledge of man's ancient handiwork, assessed in the first place by the survivals we have found, is enlarged by the written records of his possessions. It is to these that we must turn almost entirely for any estimate of the treasures of our early sovereigns, for known survivals themselves, until at least the sixteenth century, are so few as to be mere pointers to the public and private state maintained by the Kings of England. Of such survivals there are indeed only two undebatable examples – the Royal Gold Cup in the British Museum and the Coronation Spoon. The former, though sadly altered and lopped of much of its original enrichment of jewels, shows the magnificent standards to which the medieval goldsmith, though admittedly in this case French, could aspire. It is adorned in translucent enamel on sunk relief with the story of the life of St Agnes, glowing in reds, blues and greens with the intensity of cathedral glass, and was originally surmounted by a cluster of sapphires, rubies and pearls, while crestings of pearls and gold leaves ran round the cover and foot (the latter happily still remains). The cup originally belonged to Charles VI of France and subsequently passed to John, Duke of Bedford, who bequeathed it to his heir the youthful Henry VI. It is recorded in inventories of Henry VIII and Elizabeth and was subsequently presented in 1604 by James I to Juan de Velasco, Duke of Frias, the Spanish envoy for the conclusion of peace between that monarch and Philip III of Spain. Velasco presented the cup in 1610 to a convent at Medina de Pomar, where it remained till 1883, when it was sold for the convent's benefit in Paris and came into our national possession in 1892 for the sum of £8,000. Such is the history of the only surviving piece of English Royal plate earlier than the reign of Elizabeth I, with the exception of the Coronation Spoon, preserved in the Crown Jewels. This spoon, almost certainly dating from the twelfth century, is the only piece of the English Royal Regalia, apart from one fine standing salt of 1572, which is earlier than the Restoration, and we can feel reasonably sure that it was this spoon which held the sacred oil for the anointing of our English monarchs from the time of John or Henry III onwards.

Apart from these rare and fascinating survivals of the past treasures of our kings, we are driven to search ancient inventories and records for clues. The glimpses we get of medieval hoards are extremely fascinating. We know that Edward I boasted thirty-four pitchers of gold and silver for wine, ten gold chalices, ten silvergilt cups, some of them enamelled, more than one hundred silver cups, gold salts, jugs of hammered silver ornamented with figures of the king and his queen, a large silver figure of the king in surcoat and hood, and a large ewer set with pearls. The queens brought large collections of plate as part of their dower. Isabella, Edward II's wife, brought to England from France, two gold crowns set with stones, several gold and silver cups, gold spoons, fifty silver porringers, twelve great silver dishes and twelve smaller. The treasury of Henry IV contained nine mazers mounted in silver, examples of that favourite form of medieval drinking vessel formed from turned wood bowls deepened with silvergilt rims and occasionally set on feet of the same metal. Henry VIII showered plate on Anne Boleyn to the tune of nearly twelve hundred pounds' worth, and recorded items are cups, flagons, salts, chandeliers and spoons. At the famous meeting of this King with Francis I at Calais, twenty silver 'branches' (chandeliers) hung over the banqueting table suspended by long chains of the same metal. Henry is known to have commissioned designs for plate from Holbein and the latter's drawing for a gold cup for Jane Seymour, in the British Museum, is a clear indication of the virtuosity expected of fine plate at this time. The inventory of the Jewel-house under Edward VI contains a fascinating list of spoons, nearly seventy of which were of gold, some set with jewels or crystal, and many large sets of silver spoons, some with finials of types well known today from surviving examples and others whose description stimulates our imagination and the longing to see them. We read of 'xij silver spones wt gilt Columbynes at the endes', 'xxiiij spones of silver gilt whereof xij hathe Sicles at ther endes', 'xvij gilt spones wt half knoppes and Staffordes knottes at thendes' and many others which have no sur-viving counterparts.

The wedding feast of Mary and Philip of Spain was ornamented with a sideboard of nine stages or tiers, laden with gold cups and silver dishes. Elizabeth I's standards were equally lavish. Her visitations forced upon her nobles often occasioned large accretions to the Royal plate chests, as when in 1559 the Earl of Arundel entertained her at Nonsuch and presented her with the 'cupboard' of plate used by her at supper.

Eager, however, as the sovereigns were to heap up treasures for them-selves, they were equally ready to display openness of hand in their gifts to those who rendered them service, and plate offered one of the most suitable forms of largesse for the purpose. At an early date it became the custom for the plate used personally by the sovereign at the Coronation banquet to be presented as perquisites to the functionaries of the feast and this custom, at least in attenuated symbolic form, lasted down to the Coronation of George IV when the Lord Mayor, as Chief Butler, received the gold cup ceremonially presented by him to the King. This particular cup survives but with supreme national indifference was allowed to appear at auction in 1913 without any attempt made to retain it for the nation and it is now in America. A gift of plate was the usual accompaniment of any ceremonial occasion and the output of royal goldsmiths must have been extensive. A further call on the sovereign's expenditure on plate was in presentations of a diplomatic character as revealed in the history of the gold cup already described and the use James I made of it.

It is to this habit of diplomatic plate presentations that we owe the greatest surviving collection of Royal plate made to the order of English sovereigns. Although still existing it is by a quirk of fortune almost as inaccessible to us today as if it had been long melted down, for it is the collection of the Tsars of Russia still housed in the Kremlin. Fortunately in the more enlightened days of 1909 it was fully catalogued by E. Alfred Jones and we can at least turn his pages, and hope that no mad whim of the dictators of Soviet culture will consign it to the melting pot. For here are truly regal pieces, unparalleled in size and shape by any other English silver that has survived. The mouth waters at the mention of a pair of silvergilt figures of leopards seated holding shields on square fluted plinths measuring no less than thirty-six inches high which date from 1600; or silvergilt vaseshaped bottles with heavy curb chains ranging from seventeen and a half to nearly twenty-three inches overall and dating from 1580 to 1619; magnificent flagons with chased and engraved decoration fifteen and sixteen inches high of the end of the sixteenth century; standing salts of 1594 and 1611, sixteen and seventeen inches; a pair of great vaseshaped jugs of 1604 with dragon spouts and serpent handles no less than twenty-five inches overall; another pair similar of 1615; standing cups of every form and decoration; candlesticks of Charles II's reign over seventeen inches high with bases fourteen inches in diameter; all conspire to present us with a factual picture of the grandeur of plate thought worthy of passing between sovereigns.

The first gifts from England to Russia were sent in 1556 by Mary I to Ivan the Terrible in return for presents from the latter, but these have not survived, and the earliest piece is a cup of 1557 carried out by one, Anthony Jenkinson, who returned to Moscow again in 1561 and 1571. He was followed in 1581 by Sir Jerome Horsey, who took with him twenty men laden with gifts for Boris Goudounoff, which so delighted the Tsar that he spent a whole day examining the jewels, plate and armour presented to him. Two further embassies from Elizabeth were followed by Sir Thomas Smith in 1604 for James I, and John Meyrich in 1614 and 1620. Finally we should mention Charles Howard, First Earl of Carlisle, sent out by Charles II in 1663, who was provided for his personal use by royal warrant with 'a cupboard of plate of all sorts' weighing 5,333 ounces. This became his personal property on his return, as perquisites of his office.

This custom continued for Ambassadors until the end of the eighteenth century, and explains the appearance of much plate bearing the Royal arms in the possession of English families whose members have served their king in this way. This Indenture Plate, as it was called from the method of its issue, passed through the Lord Chamberlain's Office and brief details are entered in that official's Day Books, preserved in the Public Records Office. Other recipients of indenture plate were the Speakers of the House of Commons, while further origins for the existence of pieces bearing the Royal arms found in private possession are provided by christening gifts to godchildren of the sovereign and the series of gold racecups for races initiated by Queen Anne, for both of which the issue was also carefully regulated by the Lord Chamberlain and for which special pages in his Day Book are reserved. It will be seen therefore that the use of plate for Royal gifts was widely spread with the result that many examples bearing the Royal arms are met with which cannot be rightly considered as originally in the possession of the Crown.

Although it is said that the English Royal Collection of plate in Tudor times was held to be the most precious in Europe, the financial stress into which Charles I was plunged, both by the Civil War and before it, swept all away. A beginning was made in 1625 when, to raise funds for the war against Spain, a generous portion of the Regalia was pawned to Holland. This included 3,609 ounces of gold plate comprising sixteen cups set with precious stones, thirteen ewers, basins and porringers, four salts, one in the form of a ship and another known as 'The Morris Dance', twenty-nine dishes and trenchers and other treasures. In 1644 the Commons ordered all plate in the Tower to be melted down and coined, in spite of an objection from the Lords that the workmanship of the ancient plate was worth more than the metal. In 1659 the Committee of Parliament disposed of a further 5,000 ounces of plate to Alderman Backwell, goldsmith and founder of Child's Bank.

At the Restoration Charles II was faced with the necessity of providing both the regalia and plate necessary for his Coronation and also plate for the Royal palaces. But of all this, excepting the regalia and Coronation banquet plate in the Tower, only thirteen pieces now remain and this figure includes the vessels of the Chapel Royal at Whitehall. There are also certain sconces which, although they bear the cypher of William and Mary, may have had this added and could date from the end of Charles II's reign. The earliest pieces remaining in the Royal collection are a silvergilt rosewater ewer and dish hallmarked for the years 1595 and 1617, but these were acquisitions of George IV. Next in date we come to the few pieces of Charles II's reign already mentioned. There is surprisingly little fine plate of the eighteenth century. One reason for this is that a considerable quantity of plate of this time had been taken to Hanover by our sovereigns in their capacity as Elector of that State and this, on Queen Victoria's accession, was lost to this country, passing with the Kingdom of Hanover to Ernest Augustus, Duke of Cumberland. About twenty-five years ago his descendant disposed of a large selection of this English Royal plate through a London firm and the pieces have become widely spread through this country (7) and America. The pair of cups by Nicholas Clausen of 1719 come from

6

this source. The exhibition in London in 1952 of the remaining treasures belonging to the Duke of Brunswick provided an opportunity for further insight into the past possessions of the Hanoverian dynasty and included a number of interesting pieces from the workshops of English goldsmiths, as well as fine German and French plate.

The greater part of the existing Royal collection was made by George IV whose interests centred largely on ornate German pieces of the late seventeenth century, often decorated with ivory and enamels in the flamboyant style which we do not find palatable to our native taste. Both as King and earlier as Prince of Wales George IV also gave extensive commissions to Rundell, Bridge and Rundell, the Crown goldsmiths for whom Paul Storr, Benjamin Scott and Digby Smith made so many *tours-de-force*. The accounts for much of this plate reveal another reason for the paucity of earlier pieces in the Royal collection, as they include details of the old plate melted down and credited against the cost of the new pieces. In 1808, 1817 and 1823 a total sum of £13,510 was credited for the pieces melted down and since the average price allowed was slightly more than five shillings per ounce, this sum accounts for well over 50,000 ounces of plate. What the value of this holocaust would be today is in the realms of fancy but we should not be overstating the case if we imagined it to be well over one hundred thousand pounds. Much as we must deplore the apparent vandalism, we must not be overweening in our condemnation, remembering our own attitude to many of the productions of the Victorian period, and realising that in George IV's day the eighteenth century was as out-moded to his contemporaries as the former has long been to us. At least we have the consolation that the new plate provided by Rundell, Bridge and Rundell is, as we should expect, of the highest quality and includes masterpieces of the neo-Classical school which, in technical achievement, yield nothing to the work of previous periods and easily surpass any similar contemporary work from the Continent.

Great care was taken to see that the pieces were of individual character, and designs were commissioned from John Flaxman and Thomas Stothard, while in other cases the inspiration was derived from antique sculpture such as the Borghese Vase, which was the prototype for a set of wine coolers. The great majority of the pieces are in silvergilt. And here we may pause to frown on the loose thinking which so often talks of 'gold plate', whether at State banquet or City function. For in the Royal collection which we are now discussing there are only three examples of English gold earlier than 1830. Though there are other examples of later date the proportion of gold to silvergilt is probably no higher in the collection as a whole than in the earlier part of it in particular. Furthermore the total list of known pieces of old English gold plate to have survived to the present day is less than one hundred. The journalistic use of the phrase 'gold plate', although it has some sanction from the past, has often given the impression that the glitter of gold on the surface is evidence of the same metal throughout and that every piece is worth at least its equivalent weight of sovereigns. Medieval inventories are at least acquitted of this laxity of description since the metal is invariably carefully distinguished as gold, silver or silvergilt.

II

From this rapid survey of the tragedies of the past and the Royal possessions of plate to which Her Majesty is heir, we now turn to consider her personal collection which she brings with her to the throne to add to the inheritance of her forebears. The collection, from which come the pieces illustrated here, is already an extensive one. It springs in origin from the wealth of magnificent gifts made at her wedding in 1947 by all classes of her subjects throughout the Empire, strengthened by commemorative presentations offered from time to time in fulfilment of Royal functions. The pieces range in date from the years of her first Stuart ancestor down to fine modern examples commissioned by the donors, and the collection covers innumerable facets of the goldsmiths' art with a multiplicity of forms and functions. It was housed at Clarence House from 1947 till Her Majesty's removal to Buckingham Palace and was intimately related to her life there, many pieces being in daily use and the whole displayed in the glazed cases of the fine strongroom. It is our privilege now, as it were, to open the doors, pick out this or that piece, examine and admire it and move on to a fresh selection. There is real embarrassment of choice, for the illustrations have been chosen from a total of over twice the number available, which in turn was merely a broad representation of the collection as a whole. Again many of the pieces illustrated are one of a large set and the mind's eye must turn one plate into twenty-four, one candlestick into a set of six or eight, one saltcellar into twelve, to reach an estimate of the size and scope of the total collection. If this feat can be achieved the printed page may perhaps spring to life to give a glimpse of the sparkle and glow inherent in the display of this fine collection.

To be born with a silver spoon in one's mouth is not only a metaphorical suggestion of fortune by birth, but also a clear indication of the most essential piece of plate which man has invented for his needs. Among all forms of old English silver the spoon holds a special place in the eyes of collectors and justifies to many the devotion of a lifetime in its pursuit and study. Of small intrinsic value and limited opportunity for the display of the silversmith's craft, the English spoon has yet survived in larger numbers than any other form of plate. Early inventories and wills show many examples of the pride of possession in individual spoons or sets, and as we have seen from Edward vi's list distinction was carefully made in the various types devised by the silversmith. One reason, perhaps, for the survival of so many examples is the very close personal use to which the spoon was put down to the end of the seventeenth century. There is little doubt that many a spoon presented to a child at baptism was carried and used by the owner down to his death and bequeathed by him to his next of kin as a personal relic of the closest kind. The earliest reference in wills to English spoons dates from 1259 and thereafter records are numerous and varied. They have been bequeathed to individuals, colleges, churches, monasteries and municipal corporations, and in latter days to museums.

The origin of the spoon, lost in the mists of antiquity, would seem to have been the use of shells or sections of animal horn to convey food to the mouth. By Roman times the form had become standardised to a long egg-shaped bowl, attached at the narrower end to a long tapering wire-like handle. The English medieval spoon has a bowl best described as fig-shaped with a solid tapering handle either cylindrical or polygonal topped by a finial or 'knop' in a wide variety of forms — acorns, diamond points, berries, apostles, maidenheads, wild men, lions sejant, 'sealtops', balusters, and many others known only from ancient lists. Occasionally we find finials obviously made to the whim of the owner such as the fine set of six of 1506, surmounted by owls, at Corpus Christi College, Oxford, in allusion to the arms of Hugh Oldham, Bishop of Exeter, one of the College's benefactors. The most widely known type is of course the Apostle spoon, though examples earlier than about 1490 are difficult to prove. Once the next century is reached they grew strongly in popularity and lasted, with the sealtop, as the most prevalent form till the reign of Charles II, when the spoon underwent a radical change of form from which all modern types derive. There seems no reason to doubt the traditional custom of the gift of an Apostle spoon being the emblem of the saint after which the child who received it was named, but this of course can apply only to those who were so called, and then only to the male sex. The favourite saint of the donor, at least till the time of the Reformation, may well also have determined the choice, but in the case of wealthy gifts of a complete set of twelve and the Master, this further reason is surpassed.

The importance of the spoon in English silver is reflected in the fact that six Apostle spoons are the earliest pieces in Her Majesty's collection. These all bear Exeter hallmarks and range in date from about (1) 1640 to 1660, after which date few examples are known, and these mostly of a debased form and coarse workmanship. Since spoons are such essential pieces of plate we find large numbers of them surviving with the marks of provincial centres of the silversmiths' trade. In similar fashion to the Worshipful Company of Goldsmiths in London, whose charter dates from 1327, the goldsmiths in provincial towns were organised into Guilds from much the same time and in 1423 York, Newcastle-on-Tyne, Lincoln, Norwich, Bristol, Salisbury and Coventry were empowered to institute touches or distinguishing marks, for the work made in each place. Exeter, however, was not included in this Statute, though records of its goldsmiths can be traced back to the fourteenth century and many examples of sixteenth century work have survived, to which more often than not the name of the maker can be confidently ascribed since he usually adopted a form of mark in which his full name was spelt, often in a pleasingly phonetic fashion.

One of the fascinations of collecting Apostle spoons lies in the identification of the individual saints from the emblems they carry. These derive mainly from the trades of the saints or the weapons of their martyrdom. Here are St Peter with the key of Heaven, St Matthew with the wallet of his tax collector's office, St Philip with sword, St Jude with halberd, and two others whose emblems are missing. One may possibly be meant for St John who is normally represented holding a chalice in allusion to his miracle of driving the devil from a poisoned cup.

III

After spoons the most personal vessels for man's sustenance would seem to be, not plates or dishes, but something from which to quench his thirst, to judge at least from the comparative number of survivals. Here, as with spoons, cups of whatever shape or material acquired a close personal association with their owner and so were often preserved by bequest. In the medieval period men drank from horns or wooden mazer bowls, often enriched with silver or gilt mounts and although rare, examples have survived in sufficient numbers to enable us to judge the value set on these vessels. The Queen's College, Oxford, and Corpus Christi, Cambridge, have preserved fine horns of the fourteenth century. The Pusey horn, long considered to be the identical horn originally presented by King Canute to the first William Pusey as a symbol of tenure of land by 'cornage' and mounted in the fifteenth century, is in the Victoria and Albert Museum. There is another example belonging to Christ's Hospital, and a few others are in private possession. Mazers have survived in large numbers in College and Livery Company ownership, and many of these are noteworthy for finely inscribed silvergilt mounts, some made of greater importance by mounting on feet of the same metal and occasionally given covers. The ceremonial drinking of the loving cup has left us some magnificent pieces of plate, again chiefly in the possession of corporate bodies, of which the earliest survival is the fourteenth century cup at King's Lynn glowing like the Royal Gold Cup with translucent enamel panels of figures of men and women of the day.

Beer is the national beverage, and, as we should expect in a beer-drinking nation, from the sixteenth century onwards we find the covered tankard the favourite drinking vessel of the Englishman, and from the time of Elizabeth I we have, from surviving examples, a continuous picture of its development. The poor man's 'stoup' was made from wood or horn and a few early silver examples show the influence of these materials in the form given to them. There are one or two specimens remaining combining the use of horn or wood and silver, as well as German stoneware tankards enriched with silver mounts, and some of natural stone – serpentine or lava. The normal form of the Elizabethan silver tankard was that of a slightly tapering cylindrical barrel with two raised ribs, probably derived from the hoops binding the staves of the wooden prototypes, and with domed covers, the whole lavishly chased and embossed with a welter of Germanic ornament in which lions' masks, bunches of fruit and flowers and scrolling strapwork constantly occur. Other examples were decorated with engraved ornament of the same inspiration. The entry of the seventeenth century saw the tide of ornament receding and plain forms beginning to predominate. Domed covers disappeared and by the entry of Charles I's reign the vessel had assumed a severely functional form with entirely plain footless body and flat lid. The essential form remained the same throughout the century, although the foot reappeared in Commonwealth times in a curved spreading shape, to be reduced again after the Restoration to a simple moulded band strengthening the base. The plain surfaces of the barrel and cover gave ample opportunity for the display of bold engraving of arms and finely lettered inscriptions, and the interest of such pieces is much increased in this way. Her Majesty's example of 1684 is an excellent representative of this thoroughly English vessel. It bears the arms of Astley with a label for difference indicating an elder son during his father's lifetime and can be fairly certainly ascribed to Philip Astley, the eldest surviving son at that date of Sir Jacob Astley, created a Baronet in 1660, who lived until 1729, when the former became the 2nd Baronet. (3)

The eighteenth century tankards continued the traditions of functional form, with a reaction in the covers to the domed form of the sixteenth century, and as the years passed the straight sides of the barrel curved and bulged at the base into a bellied form and were usually encircled by a moulded band running round the centre. At the extreme end of this century the imitative form derived from wood returned with engraved vertical staves and moulded hooped bands, while the covers of these echoes of the past again became flat. Further than this we need not go since the large beer tankard as a contemporary form disappears and later examples are based on the earlier shapes.

Smaller drinking vessels take the form of beakers, tumbler cups and handled mugs. The beaker form we may suppose derives directly from a cup made from a section of horn, an ancestry which would account for the outward spread of the sides. This form in medieval times was used for important pieces with covers, such as the example of Christ's College, Cambridge, dating from 1507, with spreading battlemented base, but from soon afterwards the beaker became an ordinary piece of domestic plate with few or no pretensions, in which guise it has lasted down to the present. From time to time the surface was ornamented in the prevailing fashion, so that we find Elizabethan and Jacobean beakers with engraved strapwork and foliage, delicately executed, whereas under Charles I and the Commonwealth, although the motif remains much the same, the execution is coarse and scratchy. After the Restoration the beaker, like the tankard, porringer and standing cup, was decorated with large flowers and foliage in considerable relief, as (2) exemplified by the example of 1671. At this time the English silversmith was much influenced by the Dutch horticultural taste in ornament, which we may relate perhaps to the tulipomania of the Netherlands. Beakers and mugs also display the quaint mock Chinese decoration of engraved figures, birds and flowering plants which in their turn were inspired by the growing acquaintance with Chinese porcelain, chiefly imported through the Dutch East Indian trade, although curiously enough this decoration never seems to have been used on silver in Holland.

(52) The mug in pint and half-pint sizes begins to appear at the end of the seventeenth century and for the most part follows tankard forms, though throughout their development we meet with occasional deviations such as the bellied form with cylindrical neck of the sixteen-eighties, and a smaller shape under Queen Anne and George I which look exactly like undersized teacups, which, however, they certainly are not. There are indeed a few rare silver teacups surviving from Charles II's reign, straightforward imitations of the Chinese tea bowl with shallow curved sides, on rim foot, sometimes with saucer stand accompanying them. These, suitably enough, mostly have the engraved Chinoiserie decoration mentioned already, and are valuable as throwing light on the tea drinking customs of the day. They have no handles and since thin silver is highly conductive of heat we may infer that tea must then have been drunk at a rather tepid temperature if lips and fingers were to remain unhurt.

Just as silver tankards can show a derivation from wooden vessels, the quaich of Scotland, like the English mazer bowl, has an undisputed wooden origin. Examples have survived entirely of wood, of wood mounted with silver, and of silver engraved with radiating lines simulating the staves of the wooden prototypes. The quaich is essentially circular in form with shallow curving sides and usually has two diametrically opposed flat handles or lugs projecting at the rim level, though as in the present example, examples are found with three

14

handles. Quaichs have survived dating from about the mid-seventeenth century. Previous to this they were probably entirely of wood and have perished with the centuries. Her Majesty's example, of the early eigh- (13) teenth century, which is 8¼ inches in diameter, is comparatively large for these vessels, though a silver example of 1736 in the Royal Scottish Museum measures 11¼ inches. The present example has wood staves bound with two bands of withies, features which were reproduced in the silver examples, of which an echo appears in the cream bowl, Edinburgh 1815. The three wood handles are encased in silver en- (35) graved with compass-struck rosettes. There is a scalloped silver rim and in the centre a medallion or 'print' engraved with a portrait of a Highland chief, which, if it cannot be certainly identified as the Young Pretender, bears at least a close resemblance to him. It is possible that this portrait is of slightly later date than the quaich itself.

The development in the seventeenth century of the English Colonies in the West Indies introduced rum as a new drink to Englishmen which sprang to quick popularity and evoked a new vessel in which rum punch could be brewed. Early in Charles II's reign this took the form of a generously proportioned bowl with almost straight sides, with six, eight or more indentations or scallops distributed at regular intervals round the rim. These bowls acquired the name of monteiths at a fairly early date. Although the seventeenth century antiquary Anthony à Wood can be quoted as evidence for the story that this name derived from the imagined resemblance of the bowl's indented rim to the ragged cloak of a notorious Scottish adventurer of the same name, this traditional derivation should perhaps be accepted with the proverbial grain of salt. The earliest recorded monteiths are three in the possession of the Salters' Company dating from 1666, and from about 1685 a number have survived. The rims at first decorated with narrow bands of foliage later became of curving form with cherubs' heads or scroll-work applied at the higher points. An unusual example in the Green-wich Hospital plate has a cresting of dolphins. In the reign of William III the rim was made as a detachable member, and it is usually assumed that this indicates that the monteith served to bring the punch glasses to the table, their bowls hanging in the interior of the monteith, the feet suspended in the notches of the rim, and that the glasses and rim being removed, the bowl was then used for the brewing of the punch. But the existence of the earlier examples without detachable rims throws some doubt on this and we are left unsatisfied as to the exact purpose for which the detachable rim was devised. At much the same time as the latter was introduced, drop ring handles were added to the bowl, usually hanging from masks, lion or human, and this is the final form which the monteith acquired. Practically all the surviving examples were made in London though a few Dublin bowls have been re-

(5) corded. Apart from the bowl illustrated here, only two other Exeter monteiths are known to me, one by the same maker as the present one and a year earlier in date, and the other dating from 1722. Her Majesty's example is a reversion to the earlier form in having a fixed rim, though it retains the moulded band running below the indentations, which normally serves as a strengthening to both bowl and rim when the latter is detachable, and in this case demonstrates the way in which a decorative part of the design springs from a functional purpose. The

(4) shallow vertical fluting used in this monteith and the other punchbowl (which may have lost its monteith rim) is a constantly recurring motif in Queen Anne silver. It first appears on small porringers and two-handled cups at the end of the previous century and when the silver is of a thin gauge, as often at that time, adds considerably to the strength and rigidity of the piece by the reinforcing effect of the corrugations. At the same time the play of high lights on the flutes increases the scintillation of the natural metal. The treatment of the cartouche at the side, provided for crest or arms, is remarkably crisp and reveals John Elston as an accomplished technician with hammer and chaser. The similar motif on Fawdery's bowl, though up to the usual standard, is more conventionally handled and less incisive in character. By the reign of George I the monteith proper was losing its popularity and gave way to a plain punch bowl without the distinctive rim of the earlier vessel. Some later monteiths are occasionally found, but these are certainly copies or perhaps replacements of damaged originals.

16

IV

At the time that the monteith was growing in popularity the goldsmith's craft in England received an unexpected and vital stimulus by
the immigration of a large number of French Huguenots driven out of
their native country by political forces. The Edict of Nantes which had
guaranteed the French Protestants their religious freedom was revoked
by Louis XIV in 1685 and the Huguenot families fled in large numbers
to the Low Countries and England to escape the threatened persecu-
tion. The faith found its adherents very largely in the middle and trade
classes of the town, which included weavers, watch and clock makers,
goldsmiths, jewellers and others, who pursued their calling afresh in
the countries of their adoption, maintained a close liaison amongst
themselves by intermarriage and took each other's sons as apprentices in
the family businesses. This was not the first time that the crafts of
England had benefited in this way. A similar influx had occurred in
Elizabeth I's reign and the traditional hospitality of this country was
again sought. The first settlers seem to have met with little opposition
but after a time the English goldsmith, grudgingly admitting the high
standards of work of which the Huguenots were capable, closed his
ranks and endeavoured to persuade the authorities to protect his liveli-
hood by refusing to allow the latter to enter the Goldsmiths' Company.
The newly arrived foreigners, many already masters in their own right
in France, had mostly become Freemen of the Goldsmiths' Company
by redemption, but towards the end of the century a petition was made
to the Company by a number of the leading English goldsmiths against
a continuation of this, since they were forced 'to bestow much more
time and labour in working up their plate than hitherto owing to com-
petition with necessitous foreigners'. It is obvious that the Frenchmen
coupled a high standard of workmanship and design with competitive
prices and that this had made itself felt. But the country's policy was
in favour of protection of Protestant refugees and the support of any
potential enemies of Louis XIV, and nothing came of the London goldsmiths' petition. The Huguenots continued to work independently and

17

conscientiously and some of the native goldsmiths sought a different remedy by purchasing Huguenot plate, overstamping it with their own mark and retailing it as their own. Although this was probably chiefly intended to increase the formers' reputation for good work, it also argues, from the commercial aspect, that the Huguenots were ready to accept lower prices than their indigenous rivals. The first generation of Frenchmen who arrived as qualified smiths includes such names as Pierre Harache, Daniel Garnier, David Willaume from Metz and Pierre Platel who arrived in the train of William III at Brixham in 1688, but did not take up his Freedom until 1699. At the beginning of the century sons of the original refugees were received as apprentices almost always by their fellow countrymen. Among these were Augustine Courtauld, founder of the present well known textile family, and, most famous of all, Paul de Lamerie who was apprenticed to Pierre Platel in 1703.

(7)   Nicholas Clausen, another of the fraternity, entered his mark at Goldsmiths Hall in 1709 but little is known of him apart from his work which is somewhat rare. From his hand came the pair of cups and covers of 1719 bearing the arms of George I. These form part of a set of twelve of the same size and date which remained with the plate of the English sovereigns in Hanover until the dispersal, already referred to, in England of a considerable part of the whole in the 'twenties of this century, when the twelve were sold to various collectors in pairs or larger sets. The applied decoration on these cups, usually known as 'strapwork', is one of the signs manual of the Anglo-French school. Its development can be clearly traced from the 'cut-card work' formed from sheet metal cut into foliage outline and soldered flat to the surface of the bodies of porringers and other pieces, which first appears on English and French plate from about 1670 onwards. The flat sheets were later adorned with a further application of beaded tapering ribs and these in turn developed into fairly bold convex flutes, increasing the depth of modelling considerably. These plain flutes subsequently invited the application of the chasing tool and formal patterns of shells, trellis work and lambrequin panels derived from the published designs of Daniel Marot, yet another Huguenot, were used in their decoration.

By the reign of George I they had reached the form displayed by these cups. In the next decade the straps themselves were given a baluster outline and further enriched with medallion busts imitating classical cameos. The final development of the straps came with the advent of rococo style in the seventeen thirties, when the applied strapwork was given a curling outline, chased to resemble realistic leaves. The commonest use of strapwork occurs on such cups as the present though it is also employed with considerable effect on the lower part of the bodies of rosewater ewers, and jugs, and occasionally on tankards. It would be hard to find examples on the more domestic smaller pieces such as tea and coffee pots, though a limited use occurs on the stems of candlesticks.

We have noted that Clausen's work is rare, but he appears to have had a high reputation, since Peter the Great commissioned from him the remarkable silvergilt throne of 1713, which formerly stood in St. George's Hall in the Winter Palace, St Petersburg. This chair is constructed of wood entirely overlaid with silver. It stands on eagles' claw and ball feet and the handles terminate in eagles' heads. The frame is decorated with masks, scrolls and foliage and the back with a cartouche of the Imperial arms topped by a large silver crown. With it is a footstool by the same maker, with similar claw feet and decoration.

English silver furniture has rarely survived, though we know that under Charles II the lavishness of the day called forth considerable quantities. John Evelyn has recorded the exuberance of the Duchess of Portsmouth's apartments with 'great vases of white plate, tables, stands, chimney furniture, ... all of massive silver'. There are silver tables of the period remaining at Windsor Castle, and Knole, another of Queen Anne's time at Welbeck Abbey, and another by Augustine Courtauld of 1742 in Moscow; also at Knole is a pair of torcheres of 1671, and a pair of the same period at Windsor Castle, though one of these bears the gouge assay mark chiefly used on the Continent which suggests a possibly Dutch origin.

Clausen is also represented at Windsor Castle by a pair of silvergilt salt cellars or spiceboxes of rare form, dating from 1721. These resemble a sarcophagus in outline and have two centrally hinged lids, which are engraved with the arms of William and Mary; since the boxes are hall-marked for the year 1721, the earlier armorials suggest that they are a replacement of original ones of the former's reign.

The work of Paul de Lamerie is inevitably regarded as the apotheosis of the Huguenot contribution to English silver. This may be partly due to his large output, since he was at work for thirty-nine years from the entry of his mark in 1712 till his death in 1751. That he was esteemed by his contemporaries is evinced by his obituary notice in the *London Evening-Post* of August 3-6 1751 which describes him as 'particularly famous in making fine ornamental plate, and has been very instrumental in bringing that Branch of Trade to the Perfection it is now in'. The anonymous eulogist may perhaps have known Lamerie's ewer and dish at Goldsmiths Hall, commissioned in 1741, and was, in any case, un-doubtedly thinking in terms of the exuberant plate of the rococo period, since he would have thought the plain plate of thirty years earlier dis-tinctly old-fashioned. Mr Sacheverell Sitwell has hailed Lamerie as the supreme craftsman of English rococo and few would dispute this claim. But he was, in the eyes of many today, even greater in his handling of plain surfaces with his magnificent sense of proportion and balance, while in the early years of George II his restrained use of engraved and flat chased decoration is without peer. We may judge him here by two pieces which lie respectively within the first ten and last five years of his working life and present him, as he was, the acknowledged interpreter (8) of each prevailing taste. The cup and cover of 1720 convincingly de-monstrates Lamerie's innate skill in the handling of plain surfaces, relying solely on the proportion of the parts, the handles, foot and large cover finial, and the placing of the medial band of moulding. It is doubly interesting since it links its maker with one of his most impor-tant clients. It bears the arms of George Treby, M.P. for Plympton 1708, Secretary at War 1718, and Teller of the Exchequer 1724. Treby made extensive purchases from Lamerie, in 1721 and 1725, culminating in the superb toilet service now in the Ashmolean Museum, which he commissioned from the goldsmith on his marriage with Charity Hele.

Treby's plate is documented for us by the happy preservation of Lamerie's invoices for his work which give full details of the charges made for individual pieces by weight, fashion or making, and engraving, and total over £2000, a veritable fortune for the time. By a strange chance, although the present cup bears the London date letter for 1720-1 it does not appear in the invoices although a much larger cup is entered in the following terms 'Delivered a Lardge Silver Cupp & Cover weighing 176oz 14 att 6s4d pr oz ... £55.19.2, fashion 18d pr oz ... £13.15.0, engraving £1'.

A possible explanation of the omission of the present cup from this invoice is that it may have been ordered and made in the summer of 1720 (soon after the commencement of the letter for the year on May 30) and that Treby had paid for it separately. It may even have been his initial purchase from Lamerie.

The silvergilt centrepiece or épergne was made within three years of Lamerie's death and is the latest recorded example of this type of piece from his hand. It certainly justifies his obituarist's use of the phrase 'fine ornamental plate' though we must admit that technical virtuosity has outrun the artist's earlier sense of form and restraint. The chased finish of flower petals, leaves and shells achieves a naturalism of a high degree and recalls on a reduced scale the earlier virtuosity of Grinling Gibbons in his wood medium. The dishes of the épergne are removable, the smaller ones unscrewing from their branches and resting on small feet when used on their own. The branches are also detachable and when removed the sockets are concealed by small stoppers delicately chased with leaves which mask the holes.

(17)

The épergne, or 'surtout de table' as it was originally called, appeared in France about 1720, and was at first made to accommodate not only dishes for fruit, but also cruets, casters and candle branches. With such a centrepiece there was in fact little need for any other table silver and some of the early examples are of massive proportions. The earliest recorded examples by Lamerie are two of 1734. One of these which formerly belonged to Count Bobrinskoy of Moscow has two sets of three casters on separate platforms at the ends, and four candle branches, and measures thirty-two inches from end to end. The other from the Gregory heirlooms had similar sets of casters as well as two pairs of cruets in stands. Another of 1736 exhibited by Lord Portarlington in 1929 has a central dish and four smaller dishes together with four candle branches, while an example of 1738 similarly equipped but without the candle branches appeared at auction in 1919. The well-known Newdigate centrepiece of 1743 in the Victoria and Albert Museum is similar to the present example in having five dishes only with borders constituted with flower and shell motifs, which a side-by-side comparison shows to have come from the same moulds as those on Her Majesty's dishes. These six épergnes are the total number by Lamerie known to me.

The present example came from the collection of the 1st Earl of Lonsdale for whom Paul Storr made, in 1816, the plinth on which it now stands. The dishes are engraved with the former's arms and the gilding is presumably of the same date. William 1st Earl of Lonsdale was the son of the Rev. William Lowther, Bart. He succeeded his cousin James, Earl of Lonsdale, as 2nd Baron and Viscount Lowther in 1802 and was created Earl of Lonsdale in 1807. He rebuilt Lowther Castle in its present form and was a munificent patron of the arts.

Through their habit of intermarriage and apprenticeship within their own circle the Huguenot craftsmen maintained for some fifty years or more their strong individuality, but by the middle of the century the native craftsmen had absorbed much of their influence and improved their own work, while the Huguenot style became merged in the main stream of English taste, their names disappeared from the records, or became permanently anglicised and their essential contribution to English silver was over.

V

We have seen that the introduction of rum provided the silversmith with new scope in making punchbowls. Even greater were the opportunities which tea, coffee and chocolate brought in their train. For convenience we can group their introduction into this country as dating from about the mid-seventeenth century, though they remained novelties, or at best luxuries, for some considerable time. Samuel Pepys tasted his first cup of 'tee' in October 1660, and seven years later records his wife 'making of tea' in their own home, as a cure for a cold. Tea was still rare enough to be presented as a gift to Charles II in 1664 and 1666 and the East India Company did not commence its regular importation till 1669 from Java, when, no doubt in support of the home trade, its importation from Holland was forbidden. Coffee seems to have made a slightly earlier start since we find mention of Thomas Garway, tobacconist and coffeehouse keeper in Exchange Alley in 1657.

Although these beverages were reaching the country their prohibitive price restricted their popularity; tea for example cost 40/- per lb. in 1664. In consequence we find that surviving tea and coffeepots of the seventeenth century are extremely rare. The earliest known English teapot is the one of 1670 in the Victoria and Albert Museum, which would certainly be taken for a coffeepot were it not for the inscription naming its purpose which is engraved on it. This is a plain, tapering, cylindrical vessel with short straight spout at right angles to the handle and conical lid and as the inscription relates was presented to the Committee of the East India Company by George Lord Berkeley in the year it was made. The earliest coffeepot is also in the same museum. This dates from 1681 and curiously enough was also given to the East India Company by Richard Sterne. It is very close in appearance to the teapot save that spout and handle are diametrically opposite each other.

The form of these vessels can be paralleled by examples in Chinese porcelain, though these may perhaps be inspired by the silver examples, which one is inclined to see as the silversmith's evolution from the plain tankard to meet the demand for an entirely distinct and separate purpose. Other teapots of the seventeenth century show Chinese influence more strongly, as that of 1682, formerly in the collection of Mr Godfrey Williams, which is hexagonal in outline, decorated with cast panels of flowery trees and birds in relief closely akin to Oriental lacquer work.

This type of decoration also appears on a coffeepot and stand of somewhat later date, about 1720, from the Earl of Strathmore's collection. Another rare teapot dating from about 1675 is eggshaped with domed cover, decorated with matted panels, and in form resembles the wine pots of Chinese porcelain.

Although the examples surviving are few, the evidence suggests that the seventeenth century silversmith was unable to fix on any settled form for his teapots, though by the reign of William and Mary the coffeepot was standardised in the tapering cylindrical form which had appeared in the 1670 teapot. By the reign of Queen Anne the teapot too had evolved a standard shape resembling a squat pear with bulging base and domed cover completing the outline. The price of tea kept the pots small. They were accompanied by kettles of the same shape but of much larger capacity which suggests that frequent refillings of the pot were customary. These, and quite frequently the teapots, were provided with spirit lamps in open stands. It is curious by modern standards to think of the teapot being kept on the boil, but perhaps constant watering down of the contents offset the resultant stewing of the tea.

Although sugar basins and cream jugs of the Queen Anne period are known, there seems very little evidence that it was customary to order these as a service with the teapot from the same silversmith. Indeed the only recorded example of a contemporaneous service is the remarkable silvergilt one of 1712 by the Huguenot, Lewis Mettayer, belonging to the Duke of Buccleuch. After this the next in date we can quote is one of 1731-2 by Pézé Pilleau, extremely complete with teapot, coffeepot, sugar bowl, pair of tea caddies, tray, cream jug, spoon-tray, teaspoons and other pieces in shagreen case, which appeared at auction in 1934.

Tea drinking had reached Scotland at least by Queen Anne's time and a teapot with the Edinburgh hallmarks for 1708 is recorded. If anything the idea of a complete tea service appears to have grown up earlier in Scotland and examples of 1733 and 1739 are on record. But surviving examples are still extremely rare. It is therefore pleasant to be able to point to two early Scottish tea services in Her Majesty's collection although they are admittedly of a composite nature. The earlier of

the two bears the very rare Aberdeen marks. The teapot has a com- (10)
pletely spherical body which appears to have been peculiar to Scotland
and dates from about 1720-25, since Edinburgh examples of identical
form have survived dating from 1723 onwards. It bears the maker's
mark of George Robertson, admitted to the Aberdeen Incorporation of
Hammermen in 1708, while the other three pieces in the set, square
waiter, cream jug and sugar bowl are all by George Cooper, who began
his work in 1728 so that we may date them about five years later than
the teapot. The latter maker was responsible for another service, belonging to the Countess of Southesk, consisting of teapot similar to the
present example, sugar bowl with cover, cream jug and a pair of octagonal tea caddies. The other service is an Edinburgh one, the teapot (9)
by John Main 1726, while the cream boat and sugar bowl are by Robert
Lowe 1747. With the sugar bowl is a pair of sugar tongs of the rare early
form resembling fire tongs, which are, if anything, earlier than any of
the other pieces in the service.

The form evolved for the coffeepot under William and Mary remained
basically unchanged until the end of George I's reign, though variations
were introduced in the use of hexagonal or octagonal outlines. The example by Thomas Folkingham of 1713 is a fine and typical piece, (3)
demonstrating clearly the æsthetic appeal which silver of that period
makes to the taste of today. Folkingham is a worthy representative of
the native English goldsmiths who resisted the influences of their
Huguenot rivals and continued to produce honest, well-proportioned
domestic silver for normal use. Another of his coffeepots with straight
spout of 1715 is in the Victoria and Albert Museum and examples of his
teapots, candlesticks, cups, and jugs are on record. His work invariably
shows the cleanness of line and sense of balance which we have come to
associate with good examples of this period.

Following the trend of design, by the fourth decade of the eighteenth (19)
century the coffeepot had developed a tendency to show the foot as a
separate member from the body and gradually the latter bulged at the
base till the pearshaped outline appeared, reminiscent of the Queen
Anne teapot form, though naturally more elongated. The body surface

was either left plain or chased with neck and base bands — flowers, scrolls and shellwork, increasing in frequency of use and the area covered as the rococo taste for such decoration developed. At its height in the years after 1750 such chasing could cover the whole surface of body and cover while spouts were cast with birds' or dragons' heads and the main curve of the outline broken by projecting volutes. The same decoration naturally occurs on teapots which had altered radically by the mid-century from their earlier form. The pearshaped body first gave way to a near sphere, the top usually rather flattened, producing a type sometimes dubbed 'bullet shaped'; then, with the increasing curvature of form that ensued, the upper part grew larger and a body developed which was in fact an inversion of the earlier pearshape.

(15)   The teapot of 1746 displays a restrained amount of well-finished rococo decoration including a panel chased with the sun's rays bursting through a classical arch. Motifs of this type can scarcely be ascribed to the inventive fancy of the maker, whose practice then as for centuries past was to rely largely on the designs published for the express purpose of supplying craftsmen with decorative devices with which to embellish their productions and tickle the fancy of prospective clients.

Pure rococo decoration should, from its name, concern itself largely with shellwork and scrolls, though we may allow perhaps a moderate display of horticulture in the composition. The English silversmith, however, never succeeded in the former taste to the extent of the French and seems happier with a more naturalistic floral decoration which we have seen used with such high finish by Lamerie in his épergne. The

(19)   coffeepot of 1770 is typical of much of this chasing of flower sprays found on cups and covers, cream jugs, teapots, caddies and sugar bowls about this period.

The scarcity of early complete tea services has been noted and indeed English teapots are themselves comparatively rare until about 1775 by which time the best Bohea had come down in price to 6/- per lb., and tea drinking was spreading downwards in the social scale. This rarity of mid-century silver teapots may be partly accounted for by the development

26

of European porcelain, the novelty of which must have had considerable influence in fashionable circles to which tea drinking was still largely confined. It is somewhat curious that far greater numbers of tea caddies, usually in sets of a pair with matching sugar bowl, have survived from about 1720 onwards. The earliest form of the caddy was a plain oblong or octagonal canister with sliding lid or base for the insertion of the tea (often kept in condition by a lead lining) and small domed cap used for measuring it out into the pot at table. Under George I the form of the caddies changed to an oval outline while the sugar bowl was circular with a low domed cover which could be inverted on a low rim foot and served as a spoon tray if a special one was not in use. The need for this arose from the use of saucerless cups and the desire to get rid of the teaspoon after stirring the sugar in the cup. When the teapot reached its form of the reversed pear under George II the caddies and sugar bowl followed in shape and were ornamented with similar decoration, either engraved, as in the examples of 1753, with borders of rococo (20) work and coats of arms, or at slightly later date chased with the floral sprays already met with on tea and coffee pots. The oriental origin of the fragrant herb lent added point to the use of Chinese motifs and many sets are covered with panels depicting tea growing, or Chinamen in pagodas enjoying the drink. The Goldsmiths' Company possesses a pair of fine caddies by Lamerie adorned in this way.

Plainer forms of tea caddies existed at the same time such as the Edinburgh examples of 1762 by William Dempster and once the neo- (24) classical taste fostered by the Adam brothers had gained favour, the caddy and sugar vase were found to be a very suitable medium for the adaptation of classical forms of which the pair of sugar vases with the arms of Lincoln's Inn dating from 1774 are typical examples. As well as the latter, other caddies of box form were used such as the set of 1767 and 1787 (the latter not typical of its date and clearly made to match the (26) former pair) and in the 'seventies we find a charming class of cubical box engraved with Chinese characters copied from the actual wooden boxes in which the tea was imported. Later on the caddy succumbed to the prevailing taste for oval forms, while it increased in size as tea became cheaper, and is found as a single piece with partition to hold green and black brands of tea in place of the earlier pairs.

Towards the end of the century teapots, and indeed whole services, assumed an oval form often decorated with bands of engraved foliage, conventional rosettes or Greek key pattern. The oval form yielded in turn to oblong shapes, and in the new century many services are found with fluted bodies and gadrooned rims. The growth of the French Empire taste was reflected in the work of Paul Storr who made considerable use of anthemion foliage borders, serpent handles and other motifs of a mixed classical and Egyptian inspiration. Later under George IV floral decoration revived and the taste of the day for Dutch and Flemish pictures was curiously echoed by the production of tea services over-decorated with panels of peasants in bucolic scenes, derived at several removes from Teniers' kermesse subjects, which contrast strangely with the teetotal nature of the drink for which the services were intended.

Coffeepots followed the prevailing trend of decoration exemplified by the teapots. Towards the end of the eighteenth century they were given a vase form on high feet, either of oval or oblong form. Later they became cylindrical in shape and are found with spirit lamps and stands, while after 1820 the pear form of the mid-eighteenth century returned with much use of floral chasing. Victorian eclecticism produced tea and coffee services in a wide variety of form and decoration, many of a debased type, though more severe examples are met with based on classical forms, sometimes well engraved with friezes of Greek deities and warriors.

VI

Candlesticks, whether single, branched as candelabra, or hanging as chandeliers, are of as long an ancestry as any other domestic plate, though survivals before the seventeenth century are extremely rare.

The Wardrobe Accounts of Edward III contain a reference to 'vi candelabr' arg. alb. et deaur in pede' and other references occur in wills of the fifteenth century. The earliest recorded surviving silver candlestick is one of 1615, formerly in the Walker Collection, and a pair of 1618 were in the Swaythling Collection. These have open triangular feet formed of wires running between pedestal feet resembling small pepper pots. One or two pairs dating from Charles I's reign and the Commonwealth are also known and there is a large pair of 1663 chased with flowers in the Kremlin. From about 1670 sufficient examples are known to enable us to trace a continuous development of form. The majority of candlesticks of the latter part of this century are of column form on wide spreading bases, circular, square or polygonal. The columns are plain or fluted and rise from drip pans, large at first and diminishing in size as the years pass until they disappear with the introduction of baluster stems which made their regular appearance soon after 1680. The baluster remained the basic form of stem throughout the eighteenth century till the advent of the classical style reintroduced columns of the Corinthian and other orders. The earlier form of baluster stem candlestick has a square or octagonal moulded base with sunk circular centre, and this feature occasionally recurs in the eighteenth century, although the general development was towards an upward curving of the base to meet the lower knop of the stem as in the pair of candlesticks of 1713 by Gabriel Sleath. These have octagonal bases with faceted (6) borders which is repeated on the central section of the candle sockets and provides an agreeable play of light and reflections on the plain surface.

Earlier candlesticks had been fashioned from sheet silver, the bases raised by hammering and the column stems with soldered seams. The introduction of the baluster form was followed in 1697 by the raising of the standard for wrought silver from that of the coinage, 11 oz. 2 dwts. fine silver in the pound of 12 oz. to 11 oz. 10 dwts., in order to prevent the melting down of coin to provide metal for the silversmith. The softer silver of the Britannia standard, so called from the introduction of the new standard mark, lent itself more easily to cast work than hammering, and the incipient fashion for cast candlesticks was welcomed by the silversmith candlestick maker, so that examples of sticks made of sheet metal are very rare after 1697 and remained so till the advent of the classical forms about 1765.

The baluster of the stem retained its basic waisted form with shoulder knop somewhat larger than the base member, throughout the period of its use, as may be seen by the examples illustrated here, though the passing of the years brought an elaboration of the outline and the sur-

(14) face decoration. In the George II period we find a tendency to the increased use of fluting and the shaping of the stem to suggest a cluster of shafts while the bases are given a flowing outline on square, circular or polygonal figures. This was the normal pattern but reversions of entirely plain candlesticks are found also, such as the pair by George

(6) Boothby, 1745, in the middle of the rococo period. From about this time onwards for some twenty-five years the commonest ornament used on the bases and shoulders of the stems was a detached shell set at the angles and blended with bands of fluting and gadroons to give addi-

(28) tional richness of effect of which the set of 1770 are typical. This form of decoration returned in the latter years of George III, particularly on the stamped sheet silver models produced by commercial factory-like methods at Birmingham and Sheffield. The classical candlesticks of 1765 to 1780 were followed by an elegant plain form on circular bases with downward tapering stems and little decoration apart from beaded or reeded borders, to be followed in the early nineteenth century with various forms of pedestal and terminal figure stems owing allegiance to French Empire influence.

Occasional use was made at the end of the seventeenth and in the mid-eighteenth century of figures to form the stems. The Bank of England possesses a rare pair of candlesticks of 1693 by Anthony Nelme with female figures and the fashion occurs again around 1750 with Flora-like figures wreathed in flowers with uplifted arms supporting the sockets. The Huguenots enriched their candlesticks with medallion heads, panels of husks and scalework. Occasionally an English smith pro-

(11) duced similar work as in the rich set of four candlesticks by Thomas

Farrer of 1738 which, among a great variety of decorative motifs, have an interesting echo of the seventeenth century cutcard foliage patterns in small bands on the sockets and upper part of the bases. This is not achieved in applied sheet metal as was the prototype decoration, but cast on the surface with a matted background to define the shape of the leaves, and is distinctly unusual. Thomas Farrer stands high among his contemporaries for the fine finish of his work. The Goldsmiths' Company have a pair of gilt salvers by him of 1740, remarkable for the fine engraving of the Company's arms. Other noteworthy pieces by him are a gilt punch bowl of 1722 engraved with the arms of George I and the Earl of Coventry, formerly in the Hearst Collection, and another of 1725 given by the same sovereign to his godson George Lambe in that year. Candelabra, in the main, follow candlestick forms closely with the addition of the requisite number of branches related in design to harmonise with the sticks which support them. Seventeenth century examples are very rare. A pair of 1697 with three lights each has survived at Welbeck Abbey, and a single Dublin example of 1700 was in the Walker Collection. The Haberdashers' Company possess a fine three-light candelabrum of faceted octagonal form, though the branches are some ten years later in date than the stick which dates from 1714. Indeed until the mid-eighteenth century examples are rare. The three-light branch shown with the candlesticks of 1738 was not made till 1764 but with the possible exception of the flame finial in the centre is a worthy match in balance and decoration to the sticks to which it has been added.

Of particularly graceful form is the pair of silvergilt candelabra by (29) John Carter of 1771 which possess a lingering echo of the robuster rococo style of some twenty years earlier. This is principally evident in the scroll branches and their open asymmetrical finial. These have been successfully grafted on to the more restrained fluted baluster stem which rises from the square plinth of the base with a cast border of shells and reeding. The elegance of which the late eighteenth century craftsmen were capable, is much to the fore in these delightful pieces.

We should scarcely expect to find an example of a silver chandelier in any recently formed collection since these are now rarely met with except in the few cases where they have survived *in situ* in the buildings for which they were made, and where, it is hoped, they will remain. Examples of Charles II's reign have survived at Knole, and Hardwick Hall, and another is in the possession of the Duke of Buccleuch. A twelve-branched chandelier of William III's reign is at Hampton Court and a smaller one of about the same date at Chatsworth. The late Lord Desborough exhibited a pair of Queen Anne date in 1928 and another of about 1710 appeared in the dispersal of the Sneyd heirlooms in 1924. The Fishmongers' Company possesses a later example of 1752, while perhaps the most remarkable of all surviving specimens are the two by Paul de Lamerie of 1734, each with sixteen branches topped by Russian Imperial crowns, in the Kremlin Treasury.

The other form of silver candleholder, the wall sconce, is somewhat commoner. Their use was not general before the Restoration, but the Duke of Buccleuch possesses two of 1668 and four others undated, while at Knole there is a large set of twelve of 1685. The former owner has two further sets each of eight sconces dating from 1691 and 1692, while four of 1700 belong to the Duke of Devonshire. Various pairs of Queen Anne and George I period are in private possession and a late set of six by the Huguenot, Peter Archambo, of 1730, appeared in the sale of the Foley Grey heirlooms in 1921.

At Windsor Castle is a set of six (originally eight) by Charles Shelley, with the cypher of William and Mary, elaborately chased with the judgement of Solomon and another pair with the same cypher chased with lions, cherubs and other figures which are unmarked. A further set of four are of mirror form surmounted by seated cupids and the Royal crown. All these sets were refurbished with new branches or nozzles by Paul Storr in the early nineteenth century.

VII

Silver plates and dishes are mentioned in fourteenth and fifteenth century inventories but no examples earlier than the time of Elizabeth I have survived, and these are extremely rare. There is a set of twelve fruit plates of 1567 engraved with the Labours of Hercules which came from the Cotton family of Connington, passed into the collection of J. Pierpont Morgan and were sold in America in 1947 for 31,000 dollars. Another set of six of 1573 engraved with the Story of Jacob and the arms of the Montagu family were acquired in 1946 by the Victoria and Albert Museum. A further set of this period depicting the story of the Prodigal Son belongs to the Duke of Buccleuch. These sets are all remarkable examples of the engraver's art of the time and it is presumably to this fact that they owe their preservation. A much more extraordinary chance preserved a service of twenty-two dishes and plates ranging in date from 1581 to 1601. Originally the property of Sir Christopher Harris, they were buried in a field near Dartmoor in 1645 to avoid their seizure by the Parliamentary troops and having been recovered remained in the family of the original owners' descendants till they were sold in 1911 for the sum of £11,500. The service comprises fifteen dishes between $10\frac{5}{8}$ and $15\frac{1}{2}$ inches in diameter and seven plates from $8\frac{1}{8}$ to $9\frac{1}{2}$ inches. They have slightly raised centres to the wells and flat rims and were originally gilt.

The next specimens on record are twenty-two plates in Russia dating from 1639 to 1643 of which a pair of the latter date were sold by the Soviet in 1934 and passed into the collection of Sir John Noble. From the reign of Charles II onwards a number of odd plates and dishes have survived though no service of any large number, before the set of twenty-four of 1688 formerly in Sir Philip Sassoon's collection. The Earl of Methuen possessed a silvergilt dessert service of 1703 comprising twenty-four plates, ten salvers or fruit stands, and a pair of cups and covers, while the Duke of Portland owns twenty-four gilt plates of 1705 bearing the arms of Queen Anne, originally given by her to Robert Harley Earl of Oxford and Mortimer. From her reign onwards small sets of dishes and plates begin to be more common.

The majority of the dinner plate of the early eighteenth century was made with plain moulded borders and when these became out-of-date in the middle of the century large quantities were reshaped and given

33

the fashionable gadrooned rims to suit the taste of the day. These gadrooned borders remained relatively unchanged into the nineteenth century though towards the latter years of the eighteenth one meets with beaded or reeded rims as a variation. Entrée and second course

(23) dishes are little met with before the mid-eighteenth century. As we might expect they invariably have a form of gadrooned rim, either following the main shape of the dish, or given a waved outline. Perhaps

(27) the most attractive outline is that of the square or oblong dish with

(30) incurved rims which produce a shape resembling that of a cushion with curved and projecting corners. Towards the end of the century the shaping of the rims grew less popular and services were often made with the borders conforming to the main outline as in the twenty-four

(37) silvergilt dessert plates of 1795–6 engraved with the Royal arms of George III, made by the well-known firm of Robert and David Hennell.

At the end of the seventeenth century a form of shallow circular dish was evolved which was to remain in favour for over fifty years. It was in the start a favourite form of the Huguenot goldsmiths, but many examples are met with by English makers. These dishes have flat bases, upcurving sides and shaped and scalloped rims from which detached flutes run down the sides and vanish at the turn into the base. These are met with in many sizes from about four inches diameter upwards and must have been used for a variety of purposes. Sets of four and more exist, usually circular, although fanshaped examples are also known, and occasionally the larger circular dishes are given scroll handles and feet, such as a pair of 1717 which belonged to the late Lord Desborough who also owned a rare composite dessert service of 1703–5 of six circular and four fan-shaped dishes of this type. The four dishes

(12) by John Eckfourd of 1739 are excellent examples of the form which, as we have seen, lasted until nearly 1750 to be followed for a time by a transitional form which combined the fluted sides with a gadrooned border in place of the cut and scalloped rim. The arms on the dishes in Her Majesty's possession are those of Henry, third son of Sir Stephen Fox and father of Charles James Fox. They show a mark of cadency, a crescent indicating the second son, which is explained by

34

the fact that at the date the dishes were made Henry Fox was then the second surviving son of his father. Among other political posts he was Lord of the Treasury from 1743 to 1746, Secretary at War 1746–55 and Leader of the House 1762. The following year he was created Baron Holland of Foxley. His wife, who had been made Baroness Holland in her own right the year previously, was Georgiana Caroline Lennox, eldest daughter of Charles Second Duke of Richmond, whom Henry Fox had married clandestinely in 1744. Macaulay called Fox the most unpopular statesman of his time, 'not because he sinned more than any of them but because he canted less', an opinion which he perhaps derived from George II's remark on the same subject, 'I'll do him justice. I don't believe he ever did tell me a lie.' The simplicity and absence of pretension in these dishes seems to match the forthright character of their original owner.

Soup tureens do not appear to have become well established in England before the reign of George II but from about 1730 onwards are met with in a wide variety of forms dictated by the taste of the time. Mostly of oval shape on four feet with domed covers they were richly decorated as the fashion changed with strapwork, rococo scrolls, or panels of game and fish hinting at the ingredients of the soup they contained. In the Adam period they became replicas of classical urns with festoons, paterae and masks for ornament. From about 1765 they occur in sets with smaller tureens for sauce of the same design, and continued to be made in this way until well into the next century. The pair of 1808 are typical of their period. The gadrooned border which we have (44) seen as the standard element in dinner services was still popular and the plainness of the bodies is relieved by the cast lions' masks at the sides from which hang ring handles. The other pair illustrated, of 1816, are richer in effect by reason of the fluting of the bodies and feet (49) which is very similar to the decoration of tea services of the same time. The somewhat squat outline of the bodies is relieved by the upward curve of the handles which spring from leaf terminations, while the handle covers, which are detachable and bolted through the top, are similarly decorated.

Before the advent of sauce tureens, the sauceboat was the normal form of vessel for this essential accompaniment to the cook's art. The early examples of George I's reign were made with spout at each end and scroll handle at the centre of each side and are of comparative rarity. Single lipped and handled examples also occur and are met with in plain form, sometimes decorated with borders of engraving or chasing till about 1740. After this a variety of shapes and decorations is met with, and as we should expect in the rococo period, the shell motif was much in evidence since it could conveniently constitute the entire shape of the body. Elaborate examples are met with in the fourth decade, the handles and feet cast and chased as dolphins or terminal figures while the double-lipped form returns on occasions with fixed basketlike handle rising above the centre. At the same time quite plain models were also made for clients of quieter tastes or smaller pockets and these today match our demands more suitably. The pair of 1748

(16) achieve a successful contrast between the solid plain bodies and the scrolling legs resting on leaves offset by the flowing curves of the handles.

Covered entrée dishes grew in popularity as the eighteenth century neared its end and were made in large sets matching the extensive dinner services made by Paul Storr and other contemporary craftsmen in the last years of George III and the succeeding reign. Here, as in the

(41) case of the earlier uncovered dishes, gadrooned borders were common. The cover handles were usually cast in ring form chased with shells, foliage or scrollwork, but a pleasing variety and individuality was given to them on occasions by shaping them in the form of the owner's crest, when this was of a suitable nature. These dishes were often

(47) supplied with heating stands made to take hot water or sometimes heated irons and these, for economy, were usually made in Sheffield plate, though in cases where money was no object silver stands were ordered. Similar economy was effected at times by making the covers to the dishes of the imitative metal, and a certain hypocrisy may be observed when these are fitted with silver handles which bear hallmarks carefully disposed in full view to suggest that the whole cover is of the

36

same metal. For a time, as in the dishes of 1804, the oblong form was given lineally straight outline, but with the desire for richness of effect which developed about 1820 the curved outline returned with an increase   (51) of decoration in the handles.

Hash and vegetable dishes do not make any considerable appearance till the late eighteenth century, although it is sometimes difficult to know for what exact purpose some of the pieces met with were designed. The pair of plain vegetable dishes with side handles of 1809   (46) are representative of the plain functional forms produced even in periods when considerable decoration is more naturally expected. The use of heating stands for entrée dishes has been mentioned above. Earlier in the eighteenth century the need for keeping certain dishes hot was met by the use of an ingenious device – the dish cross. This has a spirit lamp in the centre round which, free to revolve to any angle,   (18) are projecting bars on which slide scroll bracket supports resting on feet usually of shell form. The combination of horizontal spread afforded by the revolving arms and the adjustable width of the brackets made a single stand available for a wide range of dishes. The need for such devices is apparent when we recall the carefree planning of Palladian architects who placed kitchens at the end of extensive wings and the dining room in the centre of the mansion with yards of stone-flagged corridor between.

Necessary to the dinner table, although not associated with the main dinner service, at least until the early nineteenth century, are the salt-cellars, cruets and casters for pepper, spices and sugar. The caster first appears in recognisable form after the Restoration and was at first of strictly functional form, shaped as a plain cylindrical box with a detachable cover of the same form pierced with large stars, trefoils and other shapes. After the turn of the next century the form became more interesting, first of pearshape and then given a waisted outline, often of octagonal form with moulded feet and borders. Under George II the casters were mounted in openwork frames in sets of three together with glass oil and vinegar bottles fitted with silver stoppers. The frames are   (31) supported on scroll and shell legs and have upright handles rising in the centre with an open ring at the top. This form persisted until the return of classical taste brought boat-shaped frames and the silver caster yielded place to a new variety of cut glass with silver covers matching the oil and vinegar bottles. A little later the stands deteriorated into oval or oblong holders with wooden bases and silver sides pierced and engraved with lattice work, festoons and foliage motifs, which appear rather unworthy descendants of the massive cruets which had preceded them. There was a return to a more dignified form at the hands of the better silversmiths such as Paul Storr, but the glass caster remained and it was left to revivalists like Robert Garrard to recall the

(53) fine work of the earlier eighteenth century.

In the medieval period the ceremonial or standing salt was one of the most important pieces of plate on which every possible ingenuity and facet of his skill was lavished by the goldsmith. A few remarkable examples have been handed down to us in the care of colleges and livery companies and there are enough examples of the Elizabethan salt still in private hands to make it possible for the wealthiest collectors to hope to acquire one. A particularly fine one of 1572 known as Queen Elizabeth's Salt, the only piece of plate of her time still in Royal possession, is among the Regalia in the Tower of London. It was the use of these important pieces as the central decoration of the high table at feasts, that gave rise to the well-known phrase of sitting 'below the salt' to indicate those who were relegated to a lower sphere outside immediate touch with the guests of first rank.

The small trencher or individual salt does not seen to have made its appearance before the seventeenth century. A few examples of circular or triangular form are known of James I's and Charles I's reign, but sets of four have not survived before 1690 and it is not till the time of Queen Anne that larger sets begin to appear. These are all of low octagonal or circular form with the sides reaching to the base and oval or circular wells for the salt. About 1720 a new form was evolved with shallow circular bowls supported on moulded bases, the former often decorated with applied palm leaves and in the next decade the bowl was given a more bellied form and set on three or four feet, often chased with lions' masks with festoons of flowers between on the bowls.

This form persisted for a considerable time and was revived again in the early nineteenth century with much the same decoration or met with in comparatively plain forms like the examples of 1804. The earlier (43) type on circular moulded foot also returned to favour, of which the set of six dating from 1806 are representative. In the latter part of the (36) eighteenth century when pierced silver was in favour, the saltcellar was usually of oval form on claw and ball feet, its sides pierced with lattice work or arabesques, and these were followed by plain solid boatshaped examples closely akin to the tureens of the period. Here we begin to see for the first time an assimilation of saltcellar form to the prevailing pattern of its contemporary dinner service plate. This is apparent again in the set of eight spanning the reigns of George IV to Victoria, with (43) shell feet and reed and tie borders with upcurving handles, exact replicas of massive soup tureens many times their size and weight, and possessing something of the charm invariably conveyed by miniature reproductions of any original.

VIII

The use of silver baskets for fruit, cakes or bread appears for some reason to be confined almost entirely to England, and our silversmiths of the eighteenth century found this form an inspiration for some of their most fanciful and elaborate productions. The idea of pierced silver baskets without handles can be traced to the days of Elizabeth I, from which one or two examples have survived. One dated 1597 is composed of pierced scalework and in the seventeenth century they were also made, decorated with a pierced pattern incorporating scrollwork and cherubs' heads. Another of 1656 is on record pierced with the floral work which was to become so popular after the Restoration. But until the eighteenth century survivals are rare, due, no doubt, to the fragility of the pierced and comparatively thin metal from which they were made. The Duke of Portland possesses a basket of 1700, circular in form and still without handle, while another of Queen Anne's reign, dating from 1711, appeared at auction in 1919. Their general use however does not seem earlier than about 1725, and owes its growth largely to the work of the second generation of Huguenots who saw in them the opportunity for elaborate piercing and cast work in which their technical abilities could be worthily displayed. Lamerie's work in this field is highly original and of great virtuosity. His recorded baskets range in date from 1724 down to the year of his death, 1751, and undoubtedly contributed much to the design of other makers. He seems to have been the originator of the use of pierced trelliswork bodies of oval form, at first with corded loop handles at the ends, as in a pair of 1724, and later with hinged central handle, the advent of which established the basic form of the silver basket which has lasted down to modern times. Whereas the basketwork design had an open rim foot similarly formed, the body in the next stage of its evolution was raised on four feet composed of the standard rococo elements of scrolls, shells, cupids' masks and other devices. This became the predominant pattern through the 'forties and 'fifties of the century. It is therefore somewhat unusual to find an example of the trelliswork form

(21)   as late as 1756, and for that pattern to emanate from a native English silversmith's hands. William Plummer's work is confined almost entirely to pierced baskets, whether of the large cake or fruit form, or of

(35)   smaller sweetmeat and sugar baskets which follow on a reduced scale the design of the larger examples. He is an example of the specialist makers of a particular class of product who had developed in the English goldsmith's trade by the mid-eighteenth century. This tendency is first noticeable among the candlestick makers of Anne's reign, to be followed shortly afterwards by the makers of casters and cruets. The taste for pierced work with its attendant demand for a particular technical skill added other specialists to the list to be followed by the makers of trays and salvers. The growth of business brought in its train a distinction between the craftsman and the retailer and there is little doubt that such specialist makers as the brothers John and William Cafe

or William Gould for candlesticks, Samuel Wood for casters, John Crouch and Thomas Hannam for salvers and trays, supplied the more fashionable West End businesses with their stock on demand and probably rarely made to private order. This division of labour was however still in its infancy and it is obvious from the great variety of pieces found from some single makers' hands that many silversmiths still worked as their own masters and offered their own wares. It is, however, a phase in the development of English silver which should be remembered. It had indeed been foreshadowed by the large goldsmith-bankers of Charles II's reign and onwards, such as Sir Richard Hoare, Sir Francis Child, and others; though in their case there is no evidence that the goldsmiths whose work they retailed were specialists in any one particular type of work. Furthermore it must not be forgotten that any master smith would have apprentices and journeymen carrying out the earlier stages of work which when finished appeared as his own production bearing his individual maker's mark.

From this digression we may return for a moment to notice that Plummer's cakebasket, already referred to, is rather surprisingly of a considerably higher standard of craftsmanship than is usually found in his work. It bears, indeed, every sign of being a specially commissioned work, a fact evinced not only by its quality but also by its slightly out-of-date nature. As we have seen, the trelliswork design had largely passed out of favour in the previous decade and this basket may have been a copy of an earlier example. It bears the arms of Langton of Langton, Lincs, the family from which came Samuel Johnson's crony, Bennett Langton, but the impalement of the arms of Kevett indicates a marriage which has not been traceable.

The rococo influence in baskets gave way in the seventh decade to a more restrained use of pierced lattice and diaperwork embellished with (34) embossed festoons of laurel to which the Adam taste added paterae and classical medallions in the prevailing style. Wirework examples also appear with applied sprays of flowers, wheat and vines. The oval form remained predominant and the piercing of the bodies became less used, until in about 1785 there is little evidence of this. Decoration was

41

then largely confined to bands of engraved geometric ornament and floral festoons of conventional flavour. These in turn lessened in use until with the turn of the century the baskets were made almost entirely plain except for gadrooned and fluted borders and feet. The circular form returned in the new century as did the use of basketwork bodies with openwork vine borders favoured by Paul Storr and others. At the same time plain bodies remained but were given a fresh note by a shaped and fluted outline. After about 1830 as with most types of work the form is lost beneath a welter of floral embossing and almost any form of decoration may be met with.

(54)

An important sphere of the craft lies in the provision of salvers and waiters used, in the nature of things, for a variety of purposes, and in the most elaborate cases designed principally as fine pieces of decorative plate to stand upright on sideboard or serving table, lending importance and an air of affluence to their surroundings. Apart however from rosewater dishes whose function is indicated by the ewers accompanying them and so can scarcely be included in this category, no firmly established examples of medieval or even sixteenth century salvers are known to have survived. A possible exception is a small plain circular salver of 1573 exhibited by the Marquess of Crewe in 1929, which bears the inscription 'On this Salver Thomas Wentworth, Earl of Strafford, was served for the last time on Wednesday, 12th May 1641 ...' A certain number of large circular dishes have survived from the second half of the seventeenth century. Lord Spencer possesses an example of 1662, twenty-six inches in diameter. From this time too date a class of oval or oblong trays generally pierced and embossed with figures and foliage that may have served for handing round fruit or other solid food but are not salvers in the accepted sense of the word. Among these are the interesting trays presented annually to the Lord Mayor with a burden of sweetmeats as a tactful 'douceur' to the first citizen of London from the Jewish Sephardic Community of Bevis Marks within his jurisdiction.

At about the mid-seventeenth century a new type of salver on spreading circular foot made its appearance as a stand for the porringer-shaped cup and cover of the time. From these, often erroneously called 'tazze', the evolution of the modern salver can be clearly traced. These stands were clearly designed to prevent the spilling of the liquid contents of the vessels they were placed beneath, and as well as porringers, have occasionally survived with tankards or in one case with a monteith bowl by the same maker, of 1689, belonging to the Apothecaries Society, a clear indication that they were intended for joint use with their accompanying vessel. At first these salvers were given a slightly dished centre in which the porringer or cup fitted, but this was later dispensed with and a flat plateau became usual. The central foot had a spreading outline and resembled the mouth of a trumpet. In this form the salver lasted into the reign of George I when an interesting transitional type was evolved in which the top unscrewed and had small feet below the rim enabling it to be used without the central foot and still prevent heat from striking through to the polished table on which it was set. The detachable central foot then became redundant and disappeared. The circular form has always remained fundamental in salvers but pleasing variations have appeared from time to time. In the early stages of its modern form from about 1720 the outline was frequently of scalloped or multifoil outline with upcurved concave rim, while square or polygonal examples occur. At the hands of the (34) Huguenots the flat centres were enlivened with borders of flat chasing, a method of hammering designs in very slight relief with small punches on matted groundwork giving a brilliant sparkle to the decorated part contrasting effectively with the sheen of the polished centres. The rims, usually cast and added to the sheet metal of the centre, were diversified with shells, scrollwork, masks and other motifs. The feet, also cast, took a variety of forms, tight scrolls, conventionalised hoofs, claw-and-ball, masks, dolphins and other fancies.

With the increasing use of gadrooned rims on dinner services, salvers were made to conform and this essential characteristic of the eighteenth century shows to great advantage on this class of plate, balanced by the focal point given to the salver by well-engraved coats of arms. The (25) rococo spirit was delightfully interpreted by the heraldic engravers, a

43

specialist class of artists in whose ranks the youthful Hogarth learnt his skill. The fantasies and lighthearted designs of which they were capable were rarely equalled by their Continental contemporaries. Influenced though they undoubtedly were by the work of such designers as Daniel Marot early in the century, and others at a.later date, they achieved delightful and highly individual pastiches of Chinamen, dragons, birds, insects, pagodas, columns, animals and peasants in unrepeated variety, making their inventions one of the minor joys of the silversmith's art. The use of pierced and cast borders appeared about the middle of the century and lasted in various forms for about two decades, to be revived

(39)   again at the beginning of the new century. The comparatively high relief in these borders catches the light in the same way as the earlier flat chasing had done.

At the end of the eighteenth century the salver shared the prevailing taste for oval forms and decoration was restricted to bands of restrained and formal pattern more closely related to those of textiles than the

(32)   metalworker's medium. Beaded borders were more frequently used than any others, as in contemporary Dutch silver, to which the English craftsmen seem most nearly allied at this period. The quiet taste of the time seems to have afforded the silversmith little opportunity for the display of any great technical virtuosity. We have to judge him, as in the early days of the same century, by his sense of proportion and the finish which he gave to his work which happily, in the best hands, showed no diminution.

Large trays for tea, or perhaps on occasions for more festive purposes, first appear at the beginning of the century. The early ones are invariably oblong in form without handles and rather curiously have survived in one or two cases without any feet. In the third decade they became magnificent productions at the hands of Lamerie and the other Huguenots, on which all the decorative devices of the smaller salvers and waiters were used on a larger scale with a necessarily increased effect of display. These large pieces disappeared from the silversmith's repertoire in the middle of the century, when the circular salver held undisputed sway, but reappeared again about 1775 when they began to

44

assume massive proportions, reaching on occasions an overall width of thirty inches. At this stage handles first appeared at the ends and were not subsequently discarded. The oval form persisted till the end of the century and was often made the vehicle for a display of fine engraving in the bright-cut technique, in which the metal is chiselled away at an angle to the main surface, producing facets to catch the light and accentuate the design which at this date was largely one of floral festoons. The new century brought back oblong trays into favour and these and (38) the oval ones were used at choice from then on. At the hands of the leading makers these trays achieved a solid dignity enhanced by the (50) crisp tooling of the decorated borders which gives them a high place in the story of English silver. They are particularly resplendent when gilt and in this guise are found with broad pierced borders of vine leaves and cast handles issuing from lion or leopard masks, making them no mean ornaments of the great houses for which their expensive nature normally predestined them. Their apotheosis is to be found in the gold example of 1821, twenty-seven inches across the handles, and 278 ounces in weight, embellished with a border composed of the orders of George IV, made by Philip Rundell for that sovereign, and still remaining at Windsor.

IX

There are many products of the silversmith's craft which do not fall into the main categories we have so far considered. Silver inkstands can be traced by a few rare survivals back to James I's reign and no doubt were used for at least a century earlier. In the reign of Charles II the casket form of standish (the contemporary word for inkstand) was evolved to which the fine example by Charles Shelley of 1685 belonging to the Treasury has lent its name as a generic title. These fine double-lidded boxes remained in favour till the reign of George II, when they were superseded by the open tray type which till then had shared the field with the Treasury inkstands. The tray form usually carries two vases for ink and pounce, powdered pumice for smoothing the paper before writing, with either a third sand-sprinkling vase, or hand bell for summoning the servant to carry away the finished missive.

The decoration of inkstands was closely allied to that of their contemporary salvers and waiters which the bases somewhat resemble, and we accordingly find the various forms of rims, flatchased and engraved borders, and varieties of feet which we have mentioned when considering salvers. About 1760 cutglass bottles for the ink and other necessaries appeared, the inkstand was given a raised latticework gallery and begins to show affinities to the cruet frames of the day. The handbell in the centre vanished and was replaced by a box for sealing wafers, often surmounted by a small taperstick for melting the wax as an alternative to the wafers. With the fall from favour of pierced fretwork as a decorative element in silver, the raised gallery disappeared towards the end of the century and the plain tray returned with depressions for pens. From then onwards the variety of individual designs (40) began to increase. Her Majesty's example of 1802 by the firm of Peter, Ann and William Bateman, successors to the well-known woman silversmith Hester, is distinctly unusual in its device of raising the taperstick above the central box on four scrolling leaf supports.

Another of the attractive forms given to small inkstands around the end of the eighteenth century was modelled on the large geographical globes popular in schoolroom and library. These have a spherical body with falling quarters concealing small glass bottles, supported in openwork stands sometimes, as in the present example, decorated with flower (34) festoons. This present piece is paralleled by another from the same maker's hand of eight years earlier, formerly in Sir Charles Jackson's collection, which has identical shell and festoon motives and the same finial, but rests on four curving claw-and-ball feet in place of the circular base shown here, which incidentally is engraved with a monthly calendar in concentric rings. These charming inventions have a feminine delicacy which seems to destine them for the boudoir bonheur-de-jour and the scribbling of brief misspelt notes of assignation, or

46

the entry into a minute pocket diary of nothing more arduous than the next ball or soirée. Larger inkstands of the Regency period, at the hands of the leading makers, were elevated to an important status. The cabinet maker's aid was sometimes called in to construct mahogany bases with drawers on which the silver inkstand fitted. Remarkably large examples occur such as that from the Fitzwilliam Collection of 1802, mounted on tortoise model feet and weighing over 200 ounces.

Silver handbells, already referred to on the inkstands of the earlier eighteenth century, are a rare and particularly attractive sideline of the English maker's craft. The example of 1830 by Robert Garrard, whom (52) we have seen in the sugar caster of 1824 using a revival of Huguenot decoration, shows him this time adapting the open applied strapwork of the same origin. Late as his place is in the development of the craft, he commands considerable respect for his intelligent and restrained use of the decorative motifs of a century earlier which reveals an eclectic taste strangely at variance with the general licence of the period. He was to continue this taste until well into the Victorian era, being par- ticularly successful in his designs for candelabra and dinner plate. The (56) work of this silversmith and the craftsmen of his firm form the con- (58) necting link in a tradition preserved by them as Crown Jewellers from the original foundation of the firm by George Wickes in the reign of George I down to the regrettable extinction of the firm as a separate entity a short time ago.

Wine coasters or slides for passing the heavy cutglass decanters round the mahogany table are first met with in the second half of the eighteenth century. Necessarily circular in shape they have solid, pierced or wirework sides and follow the prevailing styles of decoration of their particular date. From the nature of their use their decoration is often based on vine foliage and grapes as in the set of four by the firm of Rebeccah Emes and Edward Barnard of 1809. Coasters of this (53) date and style are sometimes gilt to match the large dessert services of plates, dishes, knives and forks which became a fashionable addition to the earlier white dinner services at about the turn of the century. Examples of these are the twelve by Philip Rundell of 1819

47

at Windsor Castle, pierced and embossed with boys, lions and vines.

Although the study of English silver of necessity calls for detailed consideration of the ornament used at each period and the technical skill which made its successful application possible, we must not overlook the fact that throughout its long career the silversmith was always capable of producing entirely plain pieces of a severely functional form with the precision and finish almost of a machine-made article. In such (45) cases as the cylindrical canister of 1808 we must judge the maker's skill by the exact fitting of the hinged lid and the precision of the hammering by which the body and cover are each raised from sheet metal in a single piece without seam or join of any description. The severity of the design is a perfect contrast to the vigour of the engraved heraldry which is shown at its best in such pieces as this box or the flat circular sealboxes similarly engraved with the Royal Arms, made to hold the Great Seal of the Sovereign attached to Letters Patent for Ambassadors and other holders of high office.

(55) Similar restraint and high finish are displayed on the circular bowl of 1835 with its overhanging foliage rim, another piece from Robert Garrard's workshop, who was also responsible for the appealing (57) statuette of Queen Victoria on horseback dating from five years later. Had he, one wonders, seen the earlier effort of his predecessor Paul Storr in this genre, the silvergilt figure of George III made in 1812? (48) This would seem to be one of the earliest attempts by English silversmiths at portrait modelling, a class of work which is of great rarity. Storr's technical virtuosity is lovingly applied to the smallest details such as the embroidery of the flowered vest, the ermine of the cape, shoe buckles and Collar of the Garter. Whatever the history of this piece – and it must surely have been specially commissioned – one could wish for no other possession of it than that which it now enjoys.

English art can show many attractive examples of the influence of sporting life and the silversmith has his share in this inspiration. Stirrup cups in the form of foxes' masks based on the classical 'rhyton' appeared in English silver about 1770 and were popular into the nine- (33) teenth century. The example of 1789 illustrated is typical of these light-hearted pieces. Similar cups modelled as greyhounds' heads are also found, commemorative of the achievements of a favourite animal or awarded as coursing prizes. Fox's mask cups likewise bear engraved mementoes of outstanding runs, or mottoes wishing success to the sport. Silver stirrups are considerably rarer and the example of 1746 is particularly early in date. This piece bears no inscription and arouses (52) speculation as to whether it was originally intended for a race prize — for which silver whips were sometimes given — or whether from its small size it was intended for a lady's foot, the side saddle only requiring one stirrup.

X

It has been customary among writers on English silver to consider anything produced after about 1830 as unworthy of attention and that the Victorian craftsman was incapable of original design or fine workmanship. It is indeed true that there was a rapid descent from the standards of the past, encouraged by the increasing commercialism of the business and the prevailing desire in all spheres of applied art for a maximum of lavish display. John Ruskin turned his attention to the state of affairs in his lecture 'The Political Economy of Art': 'The first idea of a rich young couple setting up house in London is that they must have new plate. Their father's plate may be very handsome but the fashion is changed. They will have a new service from the leading manufacturer and the old plate, except a few Apostle spoons, and a cup which Charles the Second drank a health in to their pretty ancestress, is sent to be melted down, and made up with new flourishes and fresh lustre. Now so long as this is the case – so long, observe, as fashion has influence on the manufacture of plate – so long you cannot have a goldsmiths' art in this country. Do you suppose any workman, worthy the name, will put his brains into a cup or an urn which he knows is to go to the melting-pot in half a score of years? He will not; you don't ask or expect it of him. You ask of him nothing but a little quick handicraft – a clever twist of a handle here and a foot there; a convolvulus from the newest school of design; a pheasant from Landseer's game cards; a couple of sentimental figures for supporters, in the style of insurance offices; then a clever touch with the burnisher, and there's your épergne, the admiration of all the footmen at the wedding breakfast, and the torment of some unfortunate youth who cannot see the pretty girl opposite to him through its tyrannous branches.' The prophet of Denmark Hill was perhaps a little hard on the pride of workmanship which many of the Victorians displayed, but his analysis of the elements of design in so much of the plate of the time comes close to the point. Nevertheless, as we have seen in the work of Robert Garrard, finely executed and restrained designs could still be obtained and the inherited traditions took rather longer to die than is sometimes supposed. By the end of the nineteenth century however there was virtually little handwrought plate being produced in this country. Such distinction as there may have been in the massiveness and naturalistic designs of the early Victorian period had degenerated further into a mass of effeminate lacy piercings and stamped patterns dignified by the traders with the names of period styles from which they were many times removed.

There was a slight resurgence of craftsmanship at the beginning of this century through the work of Omar Ramsden, though this technically able silversmith was never able to detach himself completely from the influence of the 'Nouveau Art' motif of spineless foliage forms. It was not, however, until within the last twenty years or so that English silver, largely owing to the persistent encouragement given to the craft by the Goldsmiths' Company, succeeded in re-establishing itself as a virile art form based on the traditions of the past allied to a freshness of outlook which stamps it as the child of its time. The patronage of private wealth has been replaced largely by commissions from corporate bodies, whether municipal, collegiate or commercial, and many fine pieces have resulted. Competitions for designs for specific pieces are organised by the Goldsmiths' Company and exhibitions have widened the public knowledge of what has been achieved. The three pieces here illustrated should support the claim that the goldsmiths' craft in England is a revival of importance which cannot be ignored. Harold Stabler's dish of 1937 is a worthy descendant of the fine rose-water dishes and chargers of the past, echoing in its border of conventional fountains the crispness of the Huguenots' strapwork, but of entirely original conception. The plain dish of 1936 comes closer in direct lineage to the seventeenth century which it echoes in the use of the bold and well-spaced valedictory inscription of the London, Midland and Scottish Railway. This engraving is executed, however, with a precision which the old pieces do not display, but which we naturally find acceptable in an age of machine-tools and streamlined transport. (59)

(61)

H. J. Brown's octagonal casket is another example of traditional inspiration reinterpreted by a craftsman of excellent taste. Such double-lidded boxes are met with in the early eighteenth century, such as the pair by Nicholas Clausen of 1721 already mentioned at Windsor. In the modern example the usual octagonal plan is again used and given an added grace by the subtle curvature of the sides and the delicately fluted feet and ivory finial. It is pleasant to be able to record such distinguished modern craftsmanship in Her Majesty's collection. (60)

XI

We should not expect, in a collection of English silver, designed primarily as a graceful accompaniment to modern living, to find many examples of ornate foreign plate. There are indeed only a few pieces of foreign origin in the collection altogether, and it would not be possible from these to survey the development of Continental silver in its many ramifications and clash of tastes and styles. We may, however, notice one or two pieces as a tailpiece, if only to accentuate by contrast the prevailing national taste of this country's goldsmiths.

This contrast is shown by the Italian perfume burner or vase which

(63) may probably be ascribed to Naples and dates from the eighteenth century. The goat's hoof feet occur frequently in Italian plate and are found mixed, as here, with acanthus foliage and guilloche ornament of more or less classical inspiration, blended with the less conventional projecting cherubs' masks and flower spray finial to form a showy if somewhat disproportioned composition. It would be difficult, at any period, to reconcile this ornate vase with the disciplined lines of an English piece.

(33) More pleasing to native eyes are the two small porringers with plain bodies and delicate scroll handles that own French and Channel Islands parentage. This type of bowl, dating from the late seventeenth to early eighteenth century, comes very close in taste to the English work of the period. It is indeed customary to regard the small Channel Islands pieces as a side-issue of the main family tree of English plate, although their affinities are really closer to the French as the juxtaposition of the present examples in one group will demonstrate.

(62) Equally closely related to the English monteith is the Dutch oval bowl with scalloped rim which bears the Hague marks of 1738. Dutch silver has an honourable history of development with forms and decoration that at certain times were readily adapted by our native craftsmen. The similarity of our two countries' history in their resistance to aggression coupled with a hard-headed commercial spirit developed with the rise of comparable maritime trade, and a healthy Protestantism in religious outlook, may lie perhaps behind the resemblance in our artistic impulses.

The survival in French plate of pieces earlier than the late eighteenth century is less in comparison than that of almost any other European country, due to the despotic ordinances of Louis XIV and the ravages of the Revolution. What little there is bears irrefutable witness to the superb craftsmanship of the French goldsmiths, mirrored as we have seen in the influence the Huguenots exerted in this country. The short but settled period of Napoleon's Empire allowed the production of elegant and restrained plate which has happily survived in some quantity,

(64) from which time date the set of gilt dessert plates and stands. The feet

of the latter appear to be a later addition as do the chased borders incorporating the Napoleonic emblems of bees, eagles and Imperial crowns which may perhaps date from the time of the Second Empire. The English Royal Arms beneath a ducal coronet bear a label of difference, the marks of cadency on which are, however, too small to be recognised and so make identification uncertain. It would however appear that the arms are those of one of the children of Queen Victoria into whose ownership the plates passed at some time before they entered the Earl of Lonsdale's Collection from which they passed to that of Her Majesty.

At the conclusion of this pleasant task of recording one particular section of Her Majesty's many works of art, it is with humble duty that I express my respectful gratitude at the opportunity afforded of handling and describing so many fine pieces, and the hope that my pen has not proved altogether unworthy of the honour bestowed upon it.

THE PLATES

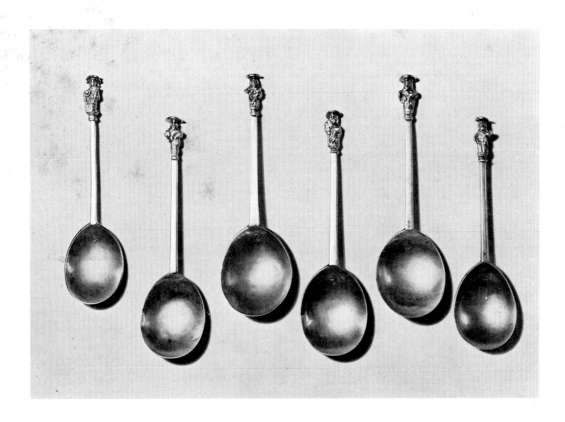

1 SIX APOSTLE SPOONS
Exeter, mid 17th century $7\frac{1}{4}$ and $7\frac{1}{2}$ in. long

Left to right

St Peter with key and rose nimbus by Edward Anthony circa 1650. Pricked with initials and the date 1660

St Matthew with wallet and rose nimbus by the same maker. Pricked with initials and the date 1652

St Philip with staff and St Esprit nimbus. Exeter mark only, circa 1650. Pricked with initials and the date 1667

St Jude with cross and St Esprit nimbus. Exeter mark only, circa 1660. Pricked with initials and the date 1663

Possibly St John (emblem worn) with St Esprit nimbus. Exeter mark only circa 1660. Pricked with initials and the date 1672

An unidentified saint with St Esprit nimbus. Exeter mark only circa 1640. Pricked with initials and the date 1647

2 PLAIN CYLINDRICAL MUG; BEAKER
Mug: by William Looker 1718 3½ in. high

Beaker: 1671. Maker's mark, probably R.D., cinque foil and pellets below 4⅛ in. high
Chased with large flowers and leaves. Pricked with the initials SN. MK. and the date 1685

3 TANKARD AND COVER; COFFEEPOT

Tankard: 1684. Maker's mark O.S. mullet and two pellets above, escallop below 7¼ in. high

Engraved with the arms of Astley with a label for difference and the date 'An. Dom. 1685'. The arms are probably those of Philip Astley, eldest surviving son of Sir Jacob Astley, 1st Baronet, who succeeded his father in 1729

Coffeepot: by Thomas Folkingham 1713 9½ in. high

With plain tapering body and domed cover. Engraved with a crest

4 CIRCULAR PUNCHBOWL
by William Fawdery 1706   11 in. diameter

Fluted body with chased foliage cartouche and lions' mask and ring handles

5 MONTEITH
by John Elston, Exeter 1708   11 in diameter

Fluted body with foliage cartouche and lions' mask and ring handles. The indented rim chased with scrolls and foliage. Engraved with the crest of Princess Elizabeth as Duchess of Edinburgh

6 TWO PAIRS OF CANDLESTICKS

Centre Octagonal faceted bases and baluster stems by Gabriel Sleath 1712 and 1713.   7 in. high
Engraved with baroque cartouche

Right and left Circular moulded bases and baluster stems by George Boothby 1745.   7¾ in. high
Engraved with crest and coronet

7 ONE OF A PAIR OF CUPS AND COVERS
by Nicholas Clausen 1719   8¼ in. high

Decorated with applied strapwork on bodies and covers and engraved with the arms of George I. These cups are part of an original set of twelve by the same maker and of the same size, which came from the collection of the Duke of Cumberland dispersed in London 1925–1926.

63

8 CUP AND COVER
by Paul de Lamerie 1720   12½ in. high

Plain body with moulded central rib and scroll handles capped with leaves. Domed cover with baluster finial. Engraved on one side with a contemporary coat-of-arms in baroque cartouche and on the other with a later coat. The contemporary arms are those of Treby quartering Grange for the Rt Hon George Treby, M.P. for Plympton 1708, Secretary at War 1718, and Teller of the Exchequer 1724. He was an important client of Paul de Lamerie and commissioned a number of fine pieces from the latter. The later arms are those of Molesworth quartering Twysden. Katharine, eldest daughter of Paul Treby Treby of Plympton married in 1817 the Rev William Molesworth. Their fourth son Walter Hele Molesworth married in 1849 Frances only daughter of Capt H. D. Twysden.

9 SCOTTISH TEA SERVICE
Edinburgh, early 18th century

Teapot of spherical form with engraved border round the lid and straight spout by John Main Edinburgh 1726; Assaymaster, Edward Penman. Engraved with the arms of Hairstans of Craigs quartering Gladstanes

Creamboat and sugar bowl with shaped rims chased with flowers and scrolls by Robert Lowe, Edinburgh 1747; Assaymaster, Hugh Gordon. Engraved with the crest of Princess Elizabeth as Duchess of Edinburgh

Sugartongs of firetong form, circa 1725

10 SCOTTISH TEA SERVICE
Aberdeen circa 1725–1730

Spherical teapot engraved round the lid with bands of foliage, by George Robertson circa 1725
6¼ in. high
Square waiter chased with a border of flowers and trelliswork, on hoof feet, engraved with a crest
8 in. square by George Cooper circa 1730
Circular sugar bowl and pearshaped cream jug on hoof feet by the same maker. Bowl 4½ in. diameter,
jug 3½ in. high

11 FOUR CANDLESTICKS AND ONE THREE-LIGHT BRANCH
The candlesticks by Thomas Farrer 1738. The branch by John Swift 1764   16½ in. high

Moulded square bases chased with satyr and female masks on trellis ground. Baluster stems chased with panels of strapwork, the shoulders similar to the bases. Sockets chased with shells and foliage. Three scroll branches with similar sockets to the sticks and with flame finial. Engraved with a coat-of-arms of six quarters and the crest of Connop

12 ONE OF FOUR DESSERT DISHES
by John Eckfourd 1739 9 in. diameter

With fluted curved sides and scalloped rims. Engraved with the arms of Fox with crescent for difference for Henry Fox, 3rd (and 2nd surviving) son of Sir Stephen Fox, created Baron Holland of Foxley 1763. Father of Charles James Fox

13 SCOTTISH SILVERMOUNTED WOOD QUAICH
Early 18th century   8¼ in. diameter

Formed of fifteen staves bound with withies. Silver rim with scalloped inner edge and silver mounts to the handles. The centre with plaque engraved with a portrait of the Young Pretender. From the Glen Lyon Collection

14 TWO PAIRS OF CANDLESTICKS

Centre: Shaped moulded circular bases and fluted baluster stems, engraved with a crest, by John Gould 1741   7¼ in. high

Right and left: Shaped moulded square bases and cluster baluster stems, engraved with a crest, by Eliza Godfrey 1750   9¼ in. high

15 TEAPOT
1746 No maker's mark   5½ in. high

Of inverted pearshape chased with panels of flowers, scrolls and sunbursts under arches, with bud finial.   Engraved with the crest of Princess Elizabeth as Duchess of Edinburgh

16 PAIR OF SAUCEBOATS
1748

Plain bodies with scalloped rims, scroll feet and handles. Engraved with initial 'E' and Royal Ducal coronet

Right

17 SILVERGILT EPERGNE WITH PLINTH
by Paul de Lamerie 1748. The plinth by Paul Storr 1816

The epergne with central oval basket and branches for four circular dishes, all with flower and scroll borders. On elaborately chased floral stand. The plinth with shell and scroll border and cupid and shell feet. Engraved with the arms of Lowther impaling Fane for William, 1st Earl of Lonsdale, so created 1807, who married in 1781 Augusta, eldest daughter of John, 9th Earl of Westmorland. From the Collection of the Earl of Lonsdale

73

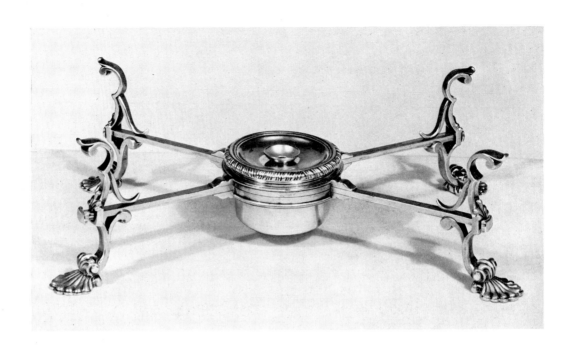

18 DISH CROSS
by Frederick Kandler 1749   10¾ in. long

Circular spirit lamp and revolving arms with sliding scroll and shell feet

19 PLAIN COFFEEPOT
by Richard Gurney and Thomas Cook 1749   9 in. high

Curved spout moulded with foliage and baluster finial

PEARSHAPED COFFEEPOT
by Charles Wright 1770 $10\frac{3}{4}$ in. high

Chased with sprays of flowers, with writhen finial

20 SET OF TWO TEA CADDIES AND SUGAR BOWL
by Thomas Heming 1753   6 and 6½ in. high

Of inverted pear form, engraved with borders of scrolls and flowers and a coat-of-arms, with cone finials. Also engraved with the crest of Princess Elizabeth as Duchess of Edinburgh. The arms are those of Fleming, Salop and Wales impaling an unidentified coat

21 OVAL CAKEBASKET
by William Plummer 1756   14¾ in. long

Pierced trelliswork body chased with quatrefoils. Basketwork rim with corded edge. Corded swing
handle and base. Engraved in a Chinese rococo cartouche with the arms of Langton, Lincs impaling
those of Kevett, with a label for difference for an eldest son

22 SET OF TWO TEA CADDIES AND SUGAR BOWL
by Samuel Taylor 1761   5½ and 5¾ in. high

Of inverted pear form. Chased with Chinese figures and sprays of flowers. Pierced floral feet and
flower finials. Engraved with the crest of Princess Elizabeth as Duchess of Edinburgh. With contemporary shagreen case

23 CIRCULAR SECOND COURSE DISH
by Thomas Heming 1762   12 in. diameter

Shaped gadroon rim
Engraved with the arms of George III and the inscription:
Presented to Her Royal Highness The Princess Elizabeth and Lieutenant Philip Mountbatten R.N. by the Members of the Royal Academy of Arts 20 November 1947

24 PAIR OF TEA CADDIES; SUGAR VASE

Tea Caddies: by William Dempster, Edinburgh 1762   5¼ in. high

Of inverted pear shape. Engraved with the crest of Princess Elizabeth as Duchess of Edinburgh

Sugar Vase: 1774   7 in. high

One of a pair of Sugar Vases engraved with the arms of Lincoln's Inn, initial and the date 1775

25 CIRCULAR SALVER
by Ebenezer Coker or Edward Capper 1766   14½ in. diameter

Shaped gadrooned rim. Engraved with two coats-of-arms on a trophy of naval weapons and
flags. The arms are those of Darby of Benington, Lincs, accollée with St Quintin, for George
Darby of Newton, Hants, Captain Royal Navy, who married Mary, daughter of Sir William
St Quintin, M.P. for Thirsk. The son of this marriage, William Thomas Darby, assumed
in 1795 the surname and arms of St Quintin

26 SET OF THREE TEA CADDIES

Two by Francis Butty and Nicholas Dumee 1767. One by William Holmes 1787

4⅝ in. high

Oblong bombé form chased with sprays of flowers and engraved with a coat-of-arms. The arms are those of Warner impaling an unidentified coat

27 ONE OF SIX OBLONG DISHES
by John Parker and Edward Wakelin 1769 10¼ in. wide

Cushion shape with gadrooned rims. Engraved with a coat-of-arms. The arms are those of Watson
with Pelham in pretence for the Hon Lewis Monson, second son of John, 1st Lord Monson, who
assumed the surname and arms of Watson upon inheriting the estates of his cousin Thomas, 3rd and
last Earl of Rockingham, and was created Baron Sondes of Lees Court, Kent in 1760. He married in
1752 Frances, second daughter of the Rt Hon Henry Pelham, and niece of the Duke of Newcastle

28 **TWO PAIRS OF CANDLESTICKS**

Centre: Two of four candlesticks on hexagonal bases and baluster stems chased with shells and fluting by Ebenezer Coker or Edward Capper 1768, 1770 and 1771   11 in. high

Right and left: Pair of candlesticks on circular bases and baluster stems chased with shells and scrolls by S. C. Younge & Co, Sheffield 1814   10½ in. high

84

29 PAIR OF SILVERGILT CANDELABRA
by John Carter 1771   14¼ in. high

On square bases with reeded and shell borders and fluted baluster stems supporting two scroll
branches with openwork finials. From the Collection of H.R.H. the Duchess of Kent

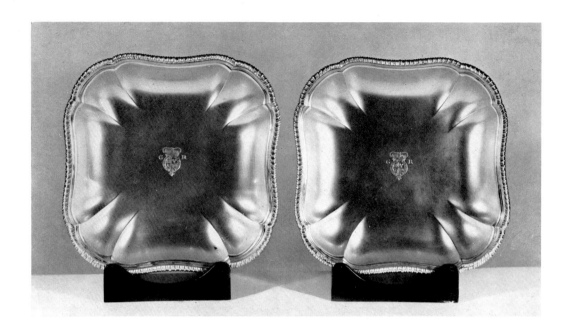

30 TWO OF FOUR SQUARE DISHES
by Thomas Heming 1771   8¾ in. square

With fluted corners and shaped gadrooned rims. Engraved with the contemporary arms of George III

Right

31 WARWICK CRUET FRAME
1771. Maker's mark ID. IM. One caster 1761. The casters 6½ and 8¼ in. high

The frame on shell feet, with ring handle and cartouche engraved with a crest. Fitted with three plain vase-shaped casters with writhen finials and two cut-glass bottles with silver stoppers

3 2 ONE OF FOUR OVAL WAITERS
by John Crouch and Thomas Hannam 1786   9¾ in. long

With bright-cut engraved borders and beaded rims. The centre engraved with a coat-of-arms

33 TWO PORRINGERS; STIRRUP CUP

Left: French circular porringer with scroll handles 4¼ in. diameter. Early 18th century

Right: Channel Islands Porringer with scroll handles 4 in. diameter. Maker's mark P.D., a crown above, probably Jersey, early 18th century

Centre: Fox's mask stirrup cup, 1789   5¾ in. long

34 INKSTAND; WAITER; SWEETMEAT BASKET

Left: Silvergilt Globe Inkstand by John Robins 1800   6 in. high   With fall down top enclosing two bottles on festooned open frame. Engraved with Royal crest, Garter motto and crest of Princess Elizabeth as Duchess of Edinburgh

Centre: Waiter by John Tuite 1727   6⅛ in. square   Plain with moulded border

Right: Sweetmeat Basket by Edward Aldridge 1765   6¼ in. wide   Pierced oval form with scroll feet and floral swing handle

35 CREAM PIGGIN; SUGAR BASKET; CREAM JUG
Left: Tub shaped cream piggin, Edinburgh 1815. Maker's mark GMH   4 in. diameter

Engraved with the inscription:
Presented to H.R.H. Princess Elizabeth (with two antique Scottish silver Teacaddies) on the occasion of her Wedding 20th November 1947 by the Braemar Royal Highland Society

Centre: Wirework Sugar Basket by William Plummer 1787   6¼ in. wide   With swing handle and blue glass liner

Right: Plain Oval Cream Jug by Robert Hennell 1793   4¾ in. high   Engraved with the crest of Princess Elizabeth as Duchess of Edinburgh

36 THREE SALTCELLARS

Left: One of a set of four circular Salts with gadrooned rims by J. Wakelin and R. Garrard 1795. Engraved with the crest of Princess Elizabeth as Duchess of Edinburgh

Centre: One of a set of twelve basket Salts with guilloche rims and handles by Robert Garrard 1867

Right: One of a set of six circular Salts with reeded rims, 1795, probably by Robert Salmon. Engraved with a contemporary crest and that of Princess Elizabeth as Duchess of Edinburgh

37 ONE OF TWENTY-FOUR SILVERGILT DESSERT PLATES
by Robert and David Hennell, eleven 1795, thirteen 1796   9⅞ in. diameter

Gadrooned rims. Engraved with the arms of George III and crest of Princess Elizabeth as Duchess of Edinburgh

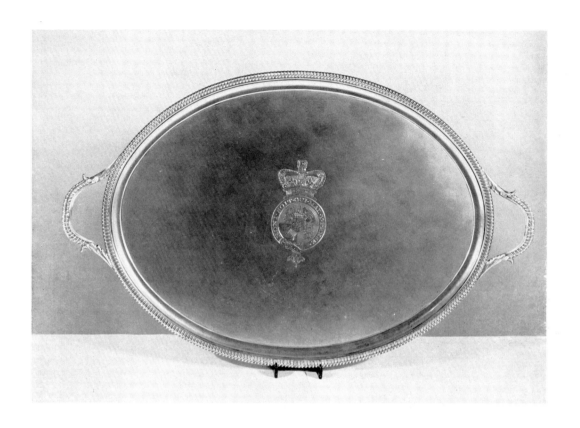

38 OVAL TRAY
by Thomas Hannam and John Crouch 1800   21½ in. long

With gadrooned border and handles. Engraved with the arms of George III

Right

39 CIRCULAR SALVER
by William Fountain 1800   16¼ in. diameter

Pierced and cast vine and mask border
Engraved with a crest in elaborate rococo cartouche

40 INKSTAND
by Peter, Ann and William Bateman 1802, oval box 1803   10½ in. long

Shaped oblong form with reeded borders, four cut-glass bottles with silver mounts and taperstick
above supported by foliage scrolls, with oval waferbox below engraved with a crest

41 **PAIR OF ENTREE DISHES AND COVERS**
by Robert Salmon 1804 $11\frac{1}{2}$ in. wide

With gadrooned borders and bull's head crest handles. Engraved with the arms of Jenkins of Charlton Hill, Salop, impaling Bullock of Arborfield, Berks. The details of the marriage are untraced. Also the crest of Princess Elizabeth as Duchess of Edinburgh and the arms of Trinity House

4 2 PAIR OF SILVERGILT DOUBLE WINECOOLERS
by Digby Scott and Benjamin Smith 1805   11 in. wide

Chased with palm foliage and a border of applied vines and coats-of-arms. Ovolo and gadrooned rims.
Handles terminating in anthemion foliage. The arms are those of Lowther impaling Fane for William,
1st Earl of Lonsdale, so created 1807, who married in 1781 Augusta, eldest daughter of John, 9th Earl
of Westmorland. From the Collection of the Earl of Lonsdale

43 THREE SALTCELLARS

Left: One of six silvergilt circular Salts with gadrooned rims, 1806. Maker's mark illegible

Centre: One of four circular Salts on three scroll feet with knurled rims by Robert Garrard 1804. Engraved with the crest of Princess Elizabeth as Duchess of Edinburgh

Right: One of eight oval Salts with reed-and-tie rims and scroll feet, six by William Eaton 1825, the others 1831 and 1837. Maker's mark GC.IC. Engraved with the crest of the Marquis of Clanricarde

44 PAIR OF SAUCE TUREENS; MUFFIN DISH AND COVER
Tureens: 1808. Maker's mark I.T. perhaps for John Thompson $7\frac{1}{8}$ in. wide

On ball feet with gadrooned rims and lions' mask and ring handles

Muffin Dish: 1809. Maker's mark TG.IW. $7\frac{1}{4}$ in. diameter
One of a pair with reeded rims and ring handles to the covers. Engraved with the crest of Princess Elizabeth as Duchess of Edinburgh

Right

45 PLAIN CYLINDRICAL BOX
1808. Maker's mark I.M. probably for John Moore   6 in. high

With hinged lid and strap clasp. Engraved with the arms of George III on the lid, and on the body with the crest of Princess Elizabeth as Duchess of Edinburgh

46 ONE OF A PAIR OF VEGETABLE DISHES AND COVERS
by Robert and Samuel Hennell 1809   8¼ in. diameter

Entirely plain except for reeded rims to the dishes. Engraved with the crest of Princess Elizabeth as Duchess of Edinburgh

47 ONE OF A SET OF FOUR ENTREE DISHES, COVERS AND PLATED
STANDS

by Thomas Robins, two 1810, two 1820   12¼ in. wide

With gadrooned, shell and foliage borders, and shell and foliage ring handles to the covers. Plated
stands on scroll feet. Engraved with the arms and crest of Ripley impaling Nottidge. The details of
this marriage are untraced

GEORGIUS TERTIUS
DEI GRATIA BRITANNIARUM REX
PATER PATRIÆ.

RUNDELL, BRIDGE, ET RUNDELL AURIFICES REGIS, &c.

48 SILVERGILT STATUETTE OF GEORGE III
by Paul Storr 1812   9⅜ in. high

Standing in Garter robes, crowned and holding sceptre. On square plinth engraved:
Georgius Tertius Dei Gratia Britannorum Rex Pater Patriae; the back with the signature: *Rundell Bridge & Rundell Aurifices Regis et Principis Walliae Londini fecerunt*

(*See also frontispiece*)

49 TWO OF FOUR CIRCULAR SAUCE TUREENS
by William Eaton 1816 5¾ in. diameter

Fluted bodies, gadrooned rims and foliage tendril handles. Engraved with the arms of Lubbock impaling Entwhistle, for Sir John William Lubbock, 2nd Baronet of Lamas, Norfolk, 1774–1840, who married in 1799 Mary, daughter of James Entwhistle of Manchester

50 OVAL TRAY
by Paul Storr 1819   22¾ in. long

Gadrooned rim chased with shells and foliage on shell feet. The centre engraved with the crest of Smith of Annsbrook, Co. Meath

5l ONE OF A PAIR OF ENTREE DISHES AND COVERS
by J. Craddock and W. Reid 1823   10⅝ in. wide

Shaped gadrooned rims and scroll foliage handles to the covers. Engraved with the arms of Johnson

52 TABLE BELL; STIRRUP; MUG
Table Bell: by Robert Garrard 1830
Applied strapwork and baluster handle

Stirrup: Pierced footplate and shoulders chased with shells and foliage   1746

Mug: 1828. Probably by William Kingdon   3⅜ in. high
With hooped bands and corded rims. Engraved with Initial 'E' and coronet

53 CASTER AND TWO OF FOUR WINE COASTERS
The vase-shaped caster chased with masks and strapwork in the style of Paul de Lamerie.
8¼ in. high by Robert Garrard 1824. Engraved with the crest of Princess Elizabeth as Duchess of Edinburgh

The wine coasters with pierced vine and grape sides by Rebeccah Emes and Edward Barnard 1809

54 OVAL CAKEBASKET
by John Fray, Dublin 1826   13 in. wide

Fluted body with gadrooned rims and handle
Engraved with the arms of Ipswich and crest of Princess Elizabeth

55 CIRCULAR BOWL
by Robert Garrard 1835   8¾ in. diameter

Overhanging foliage rim and gadrooned foot. Engraved with the Royal Cypher of William IV and the monogram of Princess Augusta Sophia with the Royal Ducal coronet

56 SET OF THREE FIVE-LIGHT CANDELABRA AND SIX CANDLESTICKS

by Robert Garrard 1866 and 1867 Candelabra 26¾ in. high Candlesticks 12 in. high

On shaped square bases and baluster stems chased with medallion heads, panels of strapwork and fluting, with guilloche borders, all in the George II taste

57 STATUETTE OF QUEEN VICTORIA
by Robert Garrard 1840   24 in. high

On horseback in riding habit with the Star of the Garter
On ebonised plinth inscribed *Victoria Regina*

58 OVAL SOUP TUREEN, COVER AND LINER
by Robert Garrard 1866   11¼ in. wide

Foliage handles and feet, and guilloche rim. Engraved with the arms of Gibraltar and crest of Princess Elizabeth as Duchess of Edinburgh

59 ROSEWATER DISH
by Harold Stabler 1937   18½ in. diameter

Decorated with panels of formalised fountains, the boss engraved with the arms of Princess Elizabeth

60 OCTAGONAL DOUBLE-LIDDED CASKET
by H. J. Brown 1947   8¼ in. wide

Plain body with outcurved sides and moulded borders. Fluted feet and ivory finial.
Engraved with the arms of Norwich and crest of Princess Elizabeth as Duchess of Edinburgh

61 ROSEWATER DISH
13½ in. diameter 1936

The rim engraved with the badge of the London, Midland and Scottish Railway and the inscription:
Ave Elizabetha, Exituri Te Salutant. MCMXLVII

62 DUTCH OVAL PUNCHBOWL
The Hague 1738. Maker's mark I.B.   14 in. wide

On moulded foot, with waisted body, indented rim and drop ring handles

Right

63 ITALIAN PERFUME BURNER
18th century, probably Naples   17¼ in. high

On tripod hoof base. The vase-shaped body decorated with cherubs' heads and chased with foliage. The cover with bunch of flowers finial

64 SIX FRENCH SILVERGILT DESSERT STANDS AND FOUR PLATES
$9\frac{1}{4}$ and $9\frac{3}{4}$ in. diameter

Paris circa 1810. The feet of the stands probably of later date. The borders chased with trellis panels and Napoleonic emblems of Imperial crowns, eagles and bees. The centres engraved with an English Royal Ducal coat-of-arms, apparently for one of the children of Queen Victoria
From the Collection of the Earl of Lonsdale